KITES

KITES

Wayne Hosking

MALLARD PRESS

A FRIEDMAN GROUP BOOK

Published by MALLARD Press
An Imprint of BDD Promotional Book Company, Inc.
666 Fifth Avenue
New York, N.Y. 10103

ISBN 0-7924-5826-5

KITES
was prepared and produced by
Michael Friedman Publishing Group, Inc.
15 West 26th Street
New York, New York 10010

Editor: Suzanne DeRouen
Art Direction: Devorah Levinrad
Designer: Paulette Cochet
Photography Editor: Christopher C. Bain

Typeset by Bookworks Plus
Color separations by Scantrans Pte. Ltd.
Printed and bound in Hong Kong by
Leefung-Asco Printers Ltd.

FOR MY FATHER-IN-LAW, HERB BIRNN.

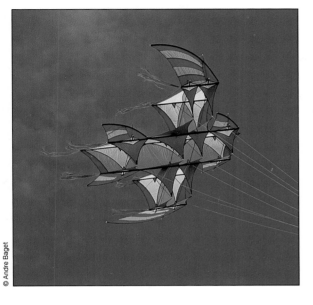

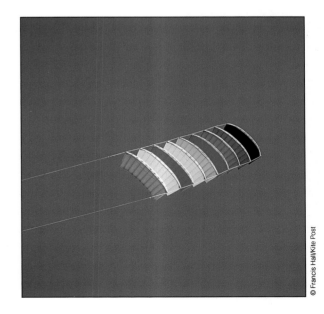

CHAPTER ONE

◆

The History of Kites

© Christopher Bain

■ Winslow Colwell's "Phaeton" Rokkaku kites. Phaeton (**OPPOSITE PAGE**), from Greek mythology, is shown falling after being struck by a lightning bolt thrown by Zeus.

12

Have you ever wondered who flew the first kite, or if its discovery was an accident or by design? Was the first kite really a coolie's hat that was caught by the wind or, as some cultures believe, a gift from the gods? Most scholars believe that kites have been around for at least two or three thousand years. Some have even attempted to explain ancient legends by associating them with kites. For example, it has been suggested that when Icarus tried to escape imprisonment by flying with waxed wings in the Greek myth, he was really carried aloft on a large kite instead. Another theory

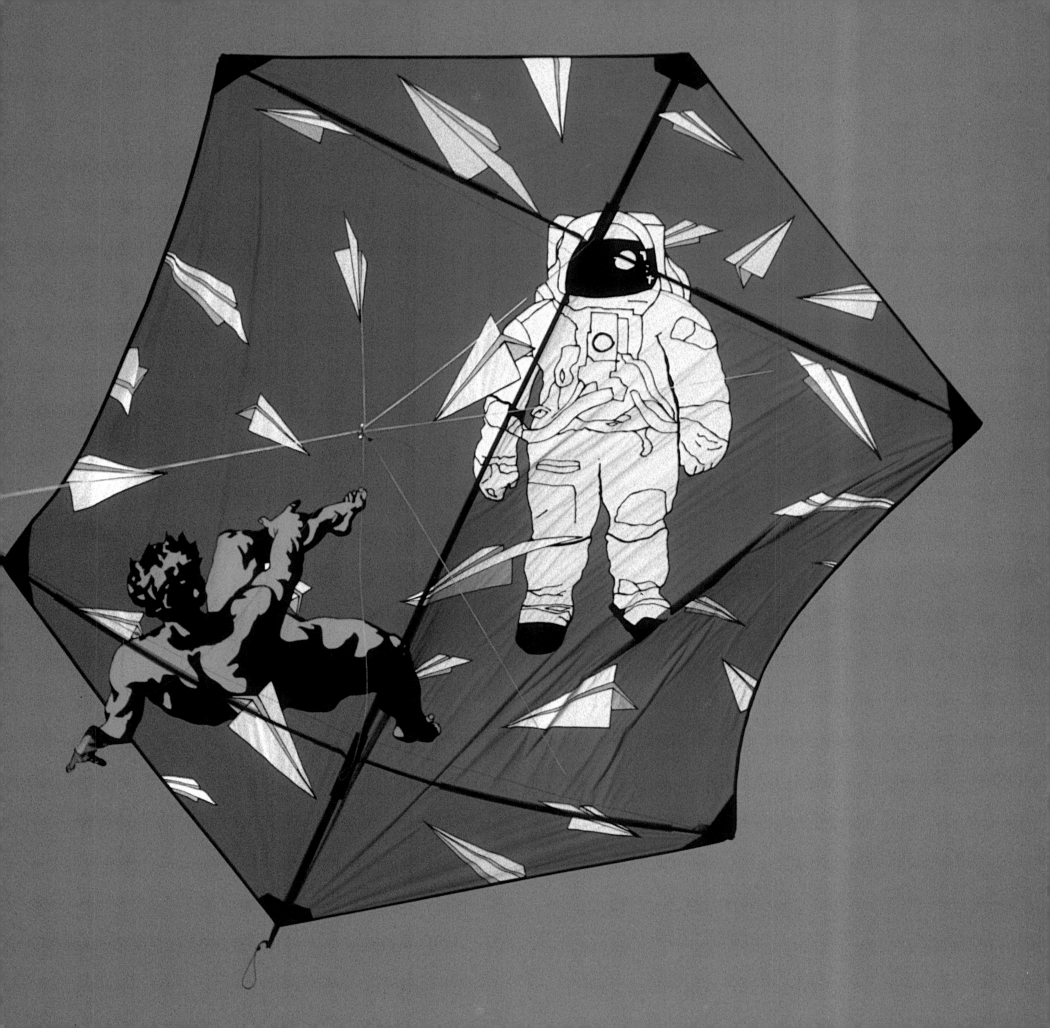

tried to explain ancient Egyptian tomb paintings by interpreting them as kites instead of tethered flying eagles. These and other theories are often cases of fact and fantasy becoming entangled in myth.

Let's begin by tracing the origins of kites and kite flying in the Far East, then discover how kites were introduced to Europe and the modern world.

China

Up until recent times, China has been credited as the originator of the kite. This is because the Chinese had an advanced civilization with an awareness of how bamboo, silk, and tools could be used for kite making. Most of all, they had the written word to record historical events. A legend from the Han dynasty (206 B.C.-A.D. 220) tells how General Han Hsin defeated General Hsiang Yu's army at Kaihsai. Han had his troops fly giant kites that were equipped with noisemakers over Hsiang's camp at night. The enemy thought that the eerie sound was made by guardian angels, warning of impending doom, and they fled in terror.

In another legend, it is said that Emperor Liang was trapped in his impregnable bastion by a besieging army. In desperation, he offered a reward to anyone who

could send a message to loyal troops waiting in another county. It was thought that a message-carrying kite would be the best answer. The kite was launched but was shot down before reaching its goal, thus allowing the emperor's enemy to learn of his helpless state.

For centuries, kites were flown with great military and religious significance. The early kites were rectangular in shape; later, forms representing birds, animals, insects, men, and dragons gained popularity. The invention of paper by Tsai Lun in the eastern Han dynasty (A.D. 25–220) led to kite making as a folk art and made it possible for all people to enjoy kite flying.

There are many customs that pertain to kite flying. Kites were flown at the spring festival of Ching Ming as talismans. At this time, families visited their ancestors' graves to pay their respects and to worship. It was believed that by flying kites, they would keep any lurking evil spirits at bay.

In the northern Sung dynasty (A.D. 960–1126), kites gained popularity, becoming a source of amusement for people of all ages. A festival called "Kite Day" was established according to a legend about a man named Haun Ching. Haun was told by a fortune-teller that on the ninth day of the ninth month a calamity would befall his household. To secure his family's safety, he was advised to take them to the hills on that day, to drink chrysanthemum wine, and to fly kites. Having done what he was told, he returned home to find all the domestic animals dead. Every year on the day that his family escaped death, people continued to travel to the hills, taking their kites. In time it was believed that a whole year's bad luck could be avoided in this way. It was also believed that

flying a high-altitude kite would reach the spirit world and carry away all the ill fate of the earthbound mortal.

Another story of the origin of Kite Day states that it was in honor of Meng Chia, who lived in the fourth century. It is said that Meng invented the kite when a gust of wind blew off his hat. Unaware of what had happened, he walked with the hat, attached by a string, still flying behind him. Whatever the origin, in one Chinese province the pastime became so popular and such a serious problem (it seems that farmers' crops were ruined by people running through the open fields flying their kites) that a law was enacted to ban kite flying.

Kite making reached its zenith in Peking, where master craftsmen built many large and exotic kites. Later the city of Tientsin became famous for its various designs, which were imitations of the original Peking style. (Today many Chinese kites found around the world come from Tientsin.) The Canton region in southern China was also famous for its style of kites. The Cantonese made their creations less flamboyant than those of Peking and included flowing tails for stability. They also believed that a kite with many sections would increase a flier's good fortune by a multiple of the number of extra sections.

During the Cultural Revolution of the 1960s, kite making was forced underground by the Red Guard. Kite flying was said to be a bourgeois practice belonging to the old order that was being destroyed. Today kites have regained favor with the Chinese and are regarded by many as a valuable cultural tradition.

© Mike Wilmer

■ Miniature Chinese kites.

East Indies and Pacific Islands

If materials and tools are the criteria for the development of the kite, it is conceivable that kites originated in the region of the East Indies and adjoining Pacific Islands. Kites there were made from natural fishing materials to make contact with the "spirit of the wind." Their kites were developed from a knowledge of sailing and sail making. Similar kites have been recorded as far away as Hawaii and New Zealand.

In some parts of the Malaysian Archipelago, Micronesia, Melanesia, and Polynesia, leaf kites were used to catch needle-nose fish. The kite allowed the fishing line,

which tended to sink, to stay on the surface of the water where the fish fed. The kite may have appeared as a hovering seabird, attracting the fish to what it thought was nearby food. The technique for fishing was to hang a line from the kite into the water. At the line's end was a baited noose or a thick loop of spider's web to entrap the fish's long snout.

The Polynesian version of the kite's origin tells of two brother gods, Rango and Tan. (Rango was the god who presided over war and peace, the dead, and kite flying.) The younger Tan challenged his brother to a kite duel, but Tan's kite became entangled in a tree while Rango's flew freely. In celebration of the event, the mortal whose kite flew the highest was honored by having his kite designated as the god Rango.

The Polynesians believed that birds were the medium through which heaven and earth could commune. The significance of the kite is reflected by its association with certain rituals in which a chief would fly a special kite in the form of a bird. Kites were also appealed to for divination. In one story the mother of two slain boys asked that a kite be used to help find their killer. Two kites were given the boy's names and flown with the appropriate ceremony. After a short while the kites hovered over the fortified village of a local chief, and a force was sent to his home. A skirmish erupted, ending with the son of the guilty chief being slain.

By the seventeenth century, when Western traders arrived in the East Indies, kite flying was well established in the region. One story tells of sailors sighting green objects fluttering above an island's shore. When they arrived, the only evidence they saw of what had transpired were bamboo-framed objects floating in the water. It was later discovered that the objects were kites that had been part of a secret ceremony to appease the wind god, the creator of typhoons. These early kites were made of palm fronds fastened to bamboo frames and flown on line made from twisted vines.

It is very possible that the Malaysians (or Pacific Islanders) and the Chinese independently discovered how to make and fly kites. There is little in common with the leaf and silk kites from these diverse regional cultures to form a correlation. It is possible to see characteristics of a later Chinese fertility-rites kite that are also common to the Malaysian *wau* kite. Their similarities, including an association with the fertility of rice fields, may be coincidental or have resulted from later contacts between the two countries.

According to a legend from Kedah, Northern Malaysia, the knowledge of how to build the *wau* kite was said to have been a gift to appease the "heavenly body." A farmer and his wife one day found an abandoned baby girl. The couple took her home and raised her with much love and care so that she grew up to be a very beautiful young lady. In time the farmer loved his adopted daughter more than anything else. His devotion was so great that it aroused the jealousy of the wife to a point where she beat the girl, who ran for her life and was never seen again. From that day forth their farm did not produce a rice harvest, and the couple fell into a great despair. They consulted Tok Nujum, a fortune teller, who explained that the girl was the "spirit of the rice field." In atonement the farmer was to construct and fly a kite in the shape of what is now called a *wau bulan*. The farmer did so, and the next year there was a harvest.

Even today, if you visit the northern *wau* kite states from April to June, you will more than likely see the tradition of making and flying *wau* kites. It is the monsoon season, a period when rice farmers and deep-sea fishermen have time to celebrate life and good fortune. Traditionally *wau* kites are shaped and decorated to gain favor when they reach the spirit region. In return for such a display of devotion, the flier hopes to be blessed with a good season and harvest.

There are over twenty styles of *wau* kites, with the *wau bulan* (moon kite) and the *wau kuching* (cat kite) being the most popular. The kite maker richly embellishes the kite's colorful glazed-tissue paper sail with cut-out patterns of flowers and ornamental foliage. A fringe of paper at the top and tassels at the sides complete the decoration. Most *wau* kites have a noisemaking bow that vibrates and fosters the belief that the kite "comes alive" once it is aloft. It is claimed that some kite fliers leave their kites flying all night, falling asleep to the soothing murmur of the hummer in their ears.

On the Malaysian west coast, kites (*layang-layang*) tend to be smaller and less elaborate than the better-known *wau*. During the kite season shops do a thriving business selling Chinese rice paper and glue, cotton twine, and dyes. These bamboo, or palm frond, framed homemade creations can generally be divided into either fighting or children's kites.

In Northern Malaysia kite fighting led to so many disputes that it was outlawed. The earliest reference to kite fighting comes from the fifteenth-century Malay Annals. Rajah Ahmad, the eldest son of Malacca's Sultan Mahmud, once flew a kite as large as a deer. By using strong fishing twine, he cleared the sky of kites. The next day the rajah went through the same process until he met Hang Isa Pantas's smaller kite. Without the rajah's knowledge, Hang had applied jungle gum and powdered glass to his twine. When the two lines crossed, the rajah's larger kite floated away on the wind.

■ **ABOVE:** Hamamatsu Machijirushi. The crane is a symbol of one of the competing neighborhoods in the traditional Hamamatsu kite battles.

■ **BELOW, LEFT:** Ismail bin Josoh making a large Wau, Kalantan, Malaysia.

■ **BELOW, RIGHT:** Megan Hosking with three Wau Bulan (moon kites). All these kites are meant to fly and are called "Terbang" (to fly).

Korea

Whatever their origin, kites spread along trade routes to the rest of Asia. The type of kite that arrived in Korea from China in the period of the Three Kingdoms (A.D. 4–645) is still flown today. The Korean fighting kite is unique because of its rectangular shape and round central vent; sizes and dimensions may vary, but the basic shape is always the same.

Like China, Korea had a dramatic history involving the military and its use of kites. In the Goryo dynasty (A.D. 918-1380), General Chue Yung was sent to a province to quell a farmers' revolt. He sailed to the region but could not land because of tall cliffs. Instead, he had his men build large kites to drop fire over the enemy's fortification. One account also claimed that he landed his soldiers at the top of the cliff with the aid of kites.

■ **BELOW, RIGHT:** Five "fancy" Indian fighter kites and a *tukkal*.

■ **BELOW:** Korean fighting kite made by Yoo Sang Roe (Seoul, South Korea).

■ **RIGHT:** Korean fighting-kite reels.

■ **OPPOSITE PAGE:** Indian fighting kites.

© Wayne Hosking

© Into The Wind

Another story concerns General Gim Yu-sin in the Silla dynasty (A.D. 595-673). During a campaign to subdue a revolt by Bi-dam and Yom-zong, a large star appeared and then fell from the sky. His troops believed that it was a bad omen and refused to fight. To regain control the next night, the general had a kite carry a fireball into the sky, where it disintegrated. Seeing the shooting star return to the sky, his troops rallied and routed the rebels.

The traditional Korean kite-flying season starts on the first day of the lunar calendar. Both children and adults fly kites after paying a New Year's visit to their elders, relatives, and neighbors. The paramount game of Korean kite flying is "fighting" for the spoils that belonged to whomever captured the freed kite. On the fifteenth day, kites with the words "bad luck away and good luck stay" are flown to ward off evil. The kites are flown as high as the line will allow and then released to carry away any bad luck. Anyone who finds one of these kites on or after the fifteenth day leaves it alone to avoid being cursed by the previous owner's bad luck.

India

Early evidence of the Indians' skills in kite flying comes from miniature paintings from the Mogul period (A.D. 1483–1530). A favorite theme was of a young lover skillfully dropping his message-bearing kite onto a rooftop and into the hands of his beloved maiden, who was held in strict seclusion from the outside world.

Today, as it has been for centuries, kite fighting is a favorite sport for many Indian men of all ages. Millions of people travel to Ahmedabad to celebrate Utran, the winter solstice. The celebrations include kite "fighting," in which opponents try to outmaneuver each other until the loser's kite line is cut by the winners. The participants purchase bundles of kites from local vendors, and over a million kites are flown and sacrificed to honor Surya, the sun god. At night small paper lanterns are raised into the sky on the lines of *tukkal* kites.

Indian fighting kites are made from tissue paper and, "like fragile butterflies," have to be flown on a soft breeze or thermal. They can be made from single colors to intricately cut designs with a "fish tail," or small tassel at the bottom. The line is made of cotton sewing thread coated with a mixture of egg white, cooked rice, dye, and powdered glass. Only about one hundred to two

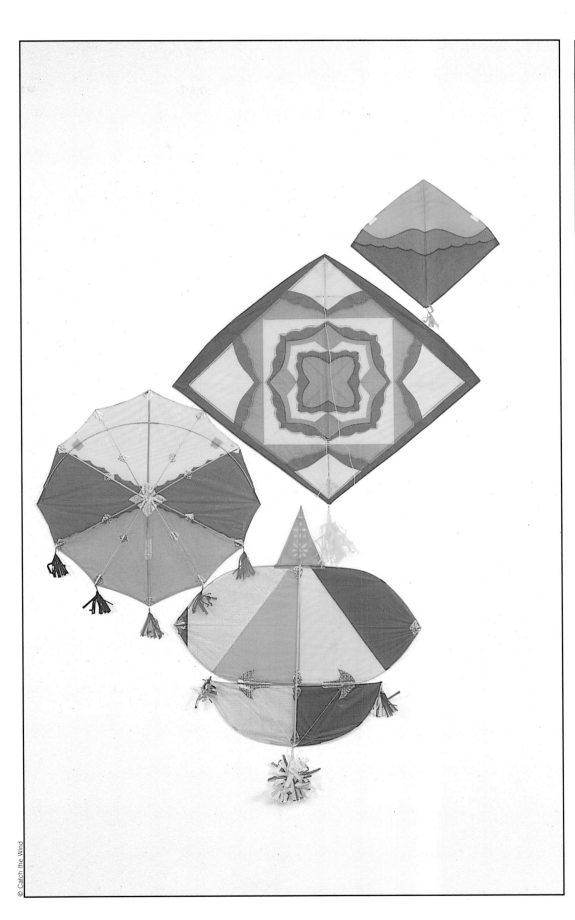

© Catch the Wind

hundred feet (30 to 60 cm) of cutting line is tied between the kite and the flying line, which is let out or retrieved with quick, rotating movements of a special reel. In kite fighting a knowledge of the wind, how to adjust a bridle, and the types of cutting line is an advantage. It is also to your advantage to know a little something about an opponent's cutting style.

Thailand

Kite flying has been practiced in Thailand as far back as anyone knows. One of the earliest legends comes from the Sukhothai period (A.D. 1238–1438) and tells about King Phra Ruang, who was a kite enthusiast. One day he was flying his kite when the string broke and it landed on the roof of a nearby palace owned by Phraya Aue. Phra Ruang decided to avoid possible embarrassment and waited until nightfall before scaling the wall to retrieve his kite. As he searched for his kite, he remembered that Phraya Aue had a beautiful daughter. Taking advantage of his situation, Phra Ruang found the girl and spent the night with her. Early the next morning he recovered his kite and slipped away.

In the late seventeenth century, King Petraja used kites to bomb a rebel stronghold in the principality of Nakhan Ratchasima. The king tied kegs of gunpowder to a large kite and flew it over the rebels to blast them into submission.

Today kite fighting in Thailand is a battle of the sexes. The combatants' kites are the dominant and aggressive "male" (chula) and the flighty and clever "female" (pakpao). The sport can be traced back to King Rammi II (A.D. 1809–1892). He often matched his chula against his courtiers' pakpao on the Phramane Ground (in Bangkok) in front of the royal palace. This is the same area where kites are flown today. In 1921, King Vajiravudh proclaimed the kite games a national sport. Both princes and commoners were able to enter their teams to compete for valuable prizes.

The star-shaped, 8.5-foot (2.5-m) chula carries three sets of bamboo barbs attached to its line to snare a female. Parts of the star shape are often referred to in human terms—head, chest, legs, and back. A chula team has ten to twenty people.

The diamond-shaped, 35-inch (.9-m) pakpao looks deceptively fragile against the larger male. Its defenses

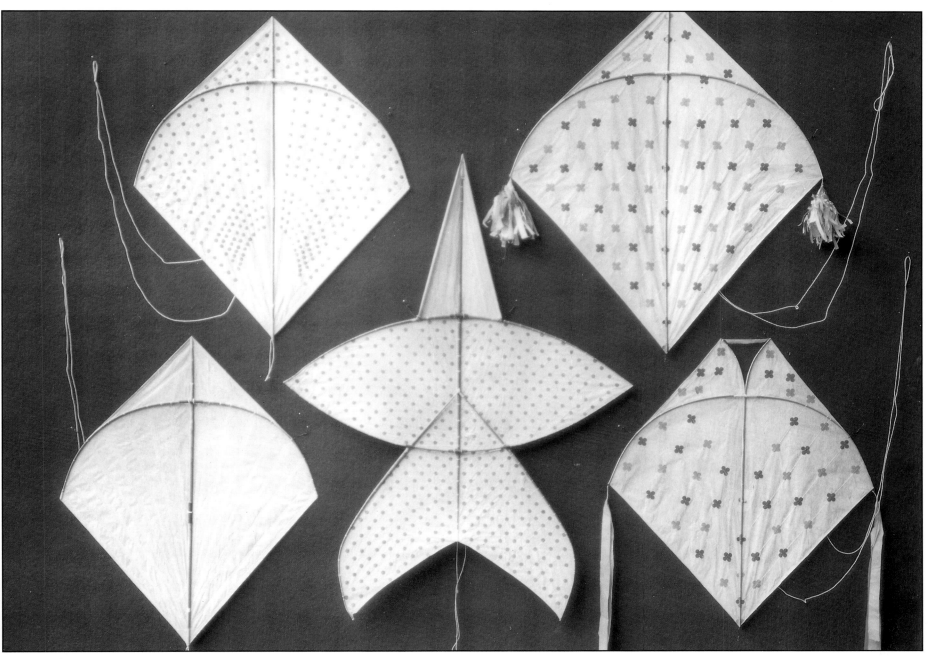

Smithsonian Institution

include excellent maneuverability, a loop of string hanging below its flying line, and a long tail. The flirty little *pakpao* is capable of darting on its cumbersome enemy with deadly accuracy. A *pakpao* team is made up of four to five people. There are five *pakpaos* to each *chula*.

At the annual tournament, held in March, the ground is divided across the center with a rope. From its upwind territory the *chula* is launched across the border into the downwind half of the field. Here the *pakpaos* flutter in "swarms like so many butterflies." The object of the game is for the *chula* to snag a *pakpao* and pull it back into male territory. In the meantime, the *pakpaos* try to use their loops or tails to capture a *chula*.

The *chula* avoids approaching *pakpaos* from below; he is the aggressor and should assume a high and proud position from which he can swoop on his prey. The *pakpao* tries to lure the larger kite into an awkward position and then darts across his path, ensnaring him with her tail or loop. Neither kite tries to destroy the other; he tries to abduct her, while she tries to capture him. It is this intricate game that makes the sport exciting for both kite fliers and spectators.

■ **OPPOSITE PAGE:** Preparing a full-sized Thai Chula (male kite) for a fighting-kite demonstration at the Aso Kite Festival (Mt. Aso, Japan).

■ **ABOVE:** Small Thai Chula (male) surrounded by four Pakpao (female) kites.

Japan

Kites arrived in Japan around the seventh century with Buddhism and the knowledge of making paper. This is very significant because paper kites played an important part in Buddhist ceremonies as talismans to avert evil spirits or as invocations for a rich harvest. Kites, like Buddhism, remained the sole domain of the privileged classes for many centuries.

Legends suggest that the Japanese, including the military, found practical uses for kites. A twelfth-century story tells of the Shogun Minamoto no Tametomo and his son, who were exiled to Oshima Island. Tametomo made a large kite and flew his son back to Honshu so that he might rally support. Their followers on the mainland then lit a fire to signal that the boy had arrived safely. This story became the basis of Bakin Takizawa's kabuki play titled *Marvelous Tales of the Crescent Moon*.

Another legend tells of a builder named Kawamura Zuiken who, in 1689, used kites to carry his workmen to the roof of the temple Zojo-ji so that they could lay tile. In contrast, the thief Kakinoki Kinsuke, in 1712, used a great kite to carry himself to the top of Nagoya Castle. A pair of gilded dolphinlike fish with tiger's heads always decorated the topmost roof of a castle to protect it from fire. Under the cover of darkness Kinsuke stole the gold scales from a dolphin. The luckless Kinsuke was captured and suffered the fate of being boiled in oil for his crime. It is said that after hearing an account of the event, the lord of Nagoya Castle was so scared of being assassinated that he banned large kites in his domain.

In Japan's Eiroku era (A.D. 1558–1569), a retainer of Iiwo Buzen-no-kami, the lord of Hikuma Castle, flew a "beetle" kite in celebration of the birth of his lord's first son, Lord Yoshihiro. This event is still celebrated today by the people of Hamamatsu with three days of kite battles. The tradition of this 400-year-old festival may be rooted in the caste system of the period. The common people had a very difficult life. Being regarded as low-class, they did not have more than a first name. A lord or samurai had the power of life and death over his people, and a man could have his head cut off for not bowing in a proper manner. Once a year these common people were allowed to enjoy themselves and to celebrate the birth of first-born males.

My first impression of a Hamamatsu kite festival was of a Middle Ages jousting tournament. Local teams (123 in

1988) try to tangle, chafe, and cut their opponents' kites from the sky. Each team has sets of kites ranging from 5 to 10 square feet (.46 to .93 sq m). The same line is used for each kite size; the stronger the wind, the smaller the kite. Sometimes holes are cut in a kite's sail so that it can be flown in strong winds. Each kite bears its team's insignia and the name of the boy in whose honor the kite is flown.

Kiting did not become universally popular in Japan until the Edo period (A.D. 1603–1868), a time of stability after the civil wars of the Middle Ages. In 1639, the Shogun Tokugawa Ieyasu imposed a "closed country" policy, cutting Japan from all ties with Europe and Asia. This national isolation was the impetus for the development of a uniquely Japanese culture including kabuki theater and *ukiyo-e* wood-block printing. These developments also created an atmosphere for kiting. The kite paintings of the period reflected their roots by mainly being reproductions of the popular characters from kabuki and *ukiyo-e* prints. The Japanese word *tako*, which is a homophone for the word meaning "octopus," derives from the custom among Edo period kite makers of displaying octopus-shaped kites in front of their shops.

■ **OPPOSITE PAGE:** Small oriental print, made largely of cut-out pieces of stamps.

■ **LEFT AND BELOW:** Miniature Japanese kites.

■ **BELOW, LEFT:** Unique kite from Okinawa, Japan, called a Yamani.

23

■ "Rising kite with Kabuki star," ukiyo-e (woodblock prints) by Kunimasa (A.D. 1773–1810). Two panels showing the type of kites flown during the height of their popularity in the Edo Period (A.D. 1603–1868).

■ OPPOSITE PAGE: A Chinese dragon kite (Weifang, China).

■ The "shoji screen"–like frame of a Machijirushi can be seen as a team carries their kite onto the flying (battle) field (Hamamatsu, Japan).

As the structure of Japanese society changed, kites were transferred from the nobles' domain into the hands of the common people. During the Edo period the government unsuccessfully tried to discourage the popularity of kites because "too many people became unmindful of their work." Travelers, mainly made up of the samurai warrior and merchant classes, carried the latest fashions from Edo to the provinces. Among their souvenirs were kites that became the basis for the development of over two hundred distinctive Japanese kite designs.

An exception was the Nagasaki *hata*, which was introduced from the East Indies. While Japan was cut off from the rest of the world, a small island in the port of Nagasaki was kept open for limited foreign contact. It was there that Dutch traders introduced a Malaysian fighting kite. Today the Nagasaki *hata* is still decorated using the Dutch flag tricolors—red, white, and blue. The *hata* is also unique among Japanese kites because the design is made of cut-and-pasted precolored paper.

Approximately one hundred kite makers resided in Edo in the middle of the eighteenth century, when kites

■ Megan Hosking, holding a small Rokkaku made by Toranosuke Watanabe (Shirone, Japan), is dwarfed by a full-sized Shirone Rokkaku.

© Mike Wilmer

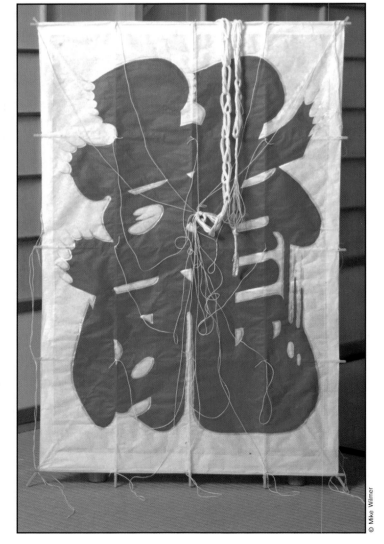

■ **ABOVE:** Rokugo Tonbi (hawk) made by Terruaki Tsutsumi (Tokyo, Japan).

■ **RIGHT:** Edo Kaku Dako with Kanji (Japanese writing) for dragon (Tokyo, Japan).

■ **ABOVE RIGHT:** A Lantern kite by Kazuho Inoue (Nagoya, Japan). One of many unusual kites on display at a Japanese kite festival (Hirosaki, Japan).

reached their height of popularity. In this century, before World War II and the bombing raids that severely damaged Tokyo, there were thirty-five kite makers' shops. Today Teizou Hashimoto (1902–) is the last of the Edo-dako masters. Hashimoto-san is the third generation of a family of kite makers who follow the *ukiyo-e-shi* style of Utagawa Kuniyoshi (1797–1861). Like most aging Japanese kite makers, he isn't passing his craft on to another generation.

Giant kites also gained in popularity in the Edo period. In 1692, a *wan-wan* kite was first flown to celebrate the reconstruction of the Rengeji Temple in the Okazaki district of Naruto City on Shikoku Island. The construction foreman, Mataemon, flew a circular kite made of fifty sheets of paper. A *wan-wan* kite was regarded as the world's largest kite until 1914 when production was stopped. It is said to have required up to two hundred men to fly it, since it was approximately 65 feet (20 m) in diameter, weighed around 5,500 pounds (2,492 kg), and was supported by thirty-five to one hundred bridle legs. If the winds proved too strong to pull or winch the kite down, it was left flying. Eventually the wind died, and the kite landed on its own.

Farmers of the Showa district were introduced to giant kites in 1730 by a traveling Buddhist priest named Joshin. He used kites as a method of divination for the forthcoming year's silkworm crop. Originally, around twenty large kites were flown at the special festival. Today, every third and fifth day of May, people from the small village of Hoshubana fly giant kites. The names of newborn sons

28

and prayers are written on paper and attached to the backs of the kites. These kites, a 1,600-square-foot (147-sq-m) and two 300-square-foot (28-sq-m) rectangular kites, are flown along the banks of the Edogawa River.

In 1736, the east bank of a drainage canal in the farming community of Shirone collapsed during a flood and was rebuilt the following year. To celebrate the canal's restoration, Mizoguchi, the lord of Shibata Castle, gave the head villager of East Shirone a very large kite. One day the kite accidentally fell on the west side of the canal, causing damage to farmhouses and the rice crop. The West Shirone farmers became infuriated and wanted revenge. In his wisdom, Lord Mizoguchi persuaded the two districts to battle with kites instead of weapons.

Today, each June, teams from the east and west banks of the Nakanokuchi River still battle with giant kites to celebrate the event. The teams fly and destroy approximately two hundred o-dako (giant 380-square-foot [35-

sq-m] rectangular kites) and 1,500 rokkaku-dako (65-square-foot [6-sq-m] hexagonal kites). In the battle, kites become secondary as lines entangle and the paper sails dissolve in the river. Each team of forty to fifty men is joined by spectators for a giant tug-of-war. The winning team gains extra points for the amount of the opponents' rope captured.

Around 1780, it is said, the sode-dako (sleeve kite) was created when, in celebration of a large catch of sardines, someone made a kite from a happi (celebration) coat. Since then, the tradition for fishermen from Chiba Prefecture has been to fly sode-dakos with family crests painted on them. The kites were flown when the fishermen set sail on long voyages and as a signal of a safe and successful return.

There are many traditions still observed in Japan that include kites. It is a way the people share the essence of their culture. Today some of the kites that are given as

■ Launching a Shirone O-dako (giant rectangular kite), Miho, Japan. Approximately two hundred O-dako kites are destroyed each June during a five-day kite battle across the Nakanokuchi River (Shirone, Japan).

© Wayne Hosking

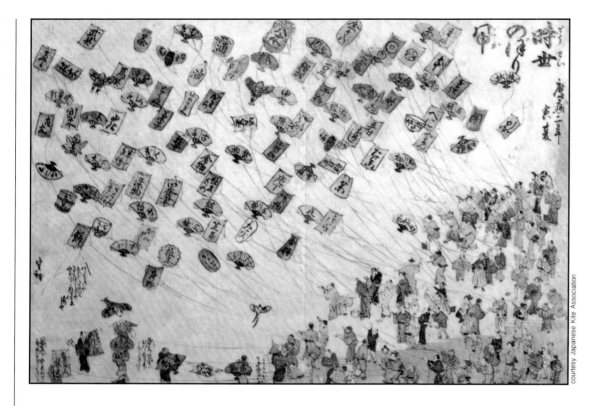

gifts are meant as tokens because they are only small representations and do not actually fly.

One of the most recognized Japanese traditions is the flying of carp wind socks, called *koinobori*. These are often mistaken as kites by Westerners. On the fifth of May, Children's Day (formerly Boy's Day), families with children attach a set of wind socks to bamboo poles in their garden. In the wind the carp appear to be swimming vigorously against the current, denoting strength and fortitude. The top pennant represents flowing water, a large black carp represents the father, a smaller red carp is for the mother, and each smaller carp represents a child in the family.

On the island of Mishima, in southwestern Japan, it is traditional for the grandfather of a first-born boy to paint a demonic face on a kite. The kite is called an *oni-yozu* (demon force), and it is hung over the baby's bed until New Year's Day, when it is taken outside and flown. The flying kite carries away all evil spirits from the house and guarantees health and happiness for the child and his family.

In the Miyagi Prefecture, kites are often called *tenbata*. Until this century people traditionally fashioned these small kites bearing their names. On New Year's Day the kites were sent aloft in the nearby mountains and the lines cut. It was believed that the freed kites would take away all evil spirits, ensuring a prosperous new year.

An ancient New Year's tradition in the Kanto district of Japan is to fly kites to the sound of bells and drums. Seers would observe and interpret the kite's movements to foretell the year's harvest and fish catch.

Fishermen in the Tohoku district used kites to decide the flow of air and thus forecast the weather for the following day. This would indicate if it was safe to set out to sea or not. They also found that it was cheaper to buy tightly wound line than the loose type that was best for fishing across rocks. Their solution was to give the new line to boys for flying their kites, which would loosen the line's twist for net making.

■ **ABOVE:** "The fast rising kites symbolize the rising cost of living," a Fushie cartoon, artist unknown (1866).

■ **RIGHT:** The first European illustration of a lozenge-shape kite (Middleburg, 1618).

Europe

Around the end of the thirteenth century, stories of kites reached Europe by way of Marco Polo and his men. European illustrations of the period show three-dimensional dragon- or pennon-shaped kites fashioned

■ Pocock's Char-volant, ca. 1822.

after Roman military banners. This type of kite was indigenous to Europe and may have been created to resemble a flying banner. An illustration from *De Nobilitatibus* of 1346 shows soldiers bombing a besieged castle with a pennon kite. By the fifteenth century, literature indicates that the dragon kite had been flattened, similar to a Thai serpent kite.

In the mid-sixteenth and seventeenth centuries, Europeans, most prominently the Dutch, found a sea route around the Cape of Good Hope and began trading throughout the East Indies. It was through their contacts with the Malay Peninsula that two kites, the arch-top and true Malay, found their way back to Europe. The new Eastern styles changed the Western view of kites, and they attracted the attention of children. They became the European arch-top and lozenge kites, which were the forerunners of today's diamond kites. These new kites were inefficient and crude in comparison to the Malay kites. They had to have long tails to make them fly. Also in the sixteenth century the English word "kite" was first used for these man-made flying objects.

By the middle of the seventeenth century, kites were regarded mainly as children's toys. Isaac Newton was said to have flown kites as a child and had improved on their design. One story had young Isaac attaching a lantern to his kites at night to light his way home. The bobbing light in the woods terrified the local farmers.

In the eighteenth century many Westerners rediscovered kites as an aid in scientific experiments. Alexander Wilson, in 1749, explored the temperatures at various altitudes using a train of kites. This precedes by three years Benjamin Franklin's famous experiment. Franklin used a kite, fashioned from a silk handkerchief, to prove that there was electricity in thunderstorms. It is amazing that he was not killed like others who have tried this hazardous act. Kites were not new to Franklin. Ben was said to have used a kite to pull himself, while floating on his back, across a pond in his youth.

In the early 1800s, Sir George Cayley, often called "the father of aviation," used kites to develop his concept of heavier-than-air flight. Cayley's first model aircraft were gliders in the form of modified arch-top kites.

Currier & Ives

Also in the nineteenth century, dirigible (steerable) kites were used to pull boats, carriages, and other objects. The most spectacular was the "char-volant" made by an English schoolteacher, George Pocock, in 1822. His creation was a carriage pulled by a pair of arch-top kites and capable of speeds up to 20 miles per hour (32 kph). The kites were flown in tandem and steered by four independent lines. This horseless rig was so unusual that it was ruled exempt from road tolls because no animals were used.

Pocock went on to experiment with kites that could lift a man and aid in the rescue of shipwrecked sailors. Other inventors also tried their hand at developing lifesaving kites. The concept was to steer a line-carrying kite from the distressed ship to shore. One noted design was by an American, Woodridge Davis, in 1894. Davis's collapsible star kite was capable of being steered by dual control lines in a wide arc.

By the last decade of the nineteenth century, "man-lifting" kites had gained popularity. Their development was the work of such men as Lawrence Hargrave, William Eddy, S. F. Cody, Alexander Graham Bell, Captain Baden-Powell, and Silas Conyne. Trains of kites by Eddy, Cody, Baden-Powell, and Conyne were developed for military use in Europe. In 1908, Cody became the first man in England to build and fly an airplane. He was later killed when one of his aircraft crashed.

Bell was also interested in creating a flying machine. He developed the tetrahedral kite and used thousands of them in some of his flight experiments. Though his "aircraft" was not successful, Bell committed himself to aviation and later financed Glenn Curtiss in a bid to perfect the airplane.

In 1890, William Eddy worked principles used in early Malay kites into his famous diamond kite design. The Eddy was a tailless kite, but it was so stable and efficient that it was used to raise meteorological payloads. The Eddy diamond kite was later replaced at the U.S. Weather Bureau's Blue Hill Observatory by the Hargrave box kite.

Lawrence Hargrave developed the box kite in 1893 while trying to invent a flying machine. He experimented with many concepts, materials, and forms. Hargrave never patented a design, preferring instead to share his results with the rest of the world.

The Wright brothers were influenced by Hargrave's work, which was documented in Octave Chanute's book *Progress in Flying Machines*. The Wrights' vision of

FPG International (both)

■ **LEFT:** Alexander Graham Bell. His research into a safe flying machine resulted in making and testing a large number of kites of varied design, the most famous being the tetrahedral kite.

■ **BELOW:** Sir Isaac Newton. He was said to have played with kites as a boy and to have improved their design.

Wilbur and Orville Wright. The Wrights first worked with kites to prove their aeronautical theories. In 1903 they became the first men to fly a flying machine, the *Wright Flyer*.

an aircraft was different from that of Hargrave and others of the period who were looking for safe, stable flight. The Wrights were looking for an unstable craft that could be controlled by steering. In 1899, they flew a 5-foot (1.5-m) "biplane" kite using four lines. This was to test a "warp" steering system that was to control the aircraft in the three axes. By changing tension on any of the four lines, the kite's wings would twist, steering the kite. The Wrights also used a wind tunnel and tethered their kite glider to test aerodynamic theories and to make calculations. In 1903, after many months of trials, the *Wright Flyer* flew and became the world's first manned flying machine.

After the development of the airplane, there is little to show that kites were used other than for recreational flying. The main styles of kites for the next fifty years were barn door, diamond, and box kites. The doldrums in kite development were broken for a short time by the World Wars I and II.

World War I created a practical use for trains of man-lifting kites. The British, French, Italian, and Russian armies all had kite units for enemy observations at the battle front. The introduction of military airplanes quickly made these units obsolete. The German Navy used man-lifting box kites to increase their viewing range from surface-cruising submarines.

In the Second World War, German Navy observers were again carried aloft from surfaced submarines, this time in highly maneuverable rotating-wing gyroplane kites.

Smithsonian Institution

© Christopher Bain

The U.S. Navy found uses for such kites as Harry Saul's barrage kite, the Gibson-Girl box kite, and Paul Garber's target kite. Harry Saul's kites were meant to be flown behind merchant ships, from cables, to deter enemy dive bombers. The kite was a modified Hargrave box design with a wing span of 20 feet (6 m).

In 1942, Lieutenant Commander Paul Garber was a recognition officer on the carrier USS *Block Island*. He was assigned to the U.S. Navy's Special Devices Division to make aircraft recognition models. Garber had been flying kites since the age of five and had written a book, *Kites and Kite Flying*, for the Boy Scouts in 1931. One day he made a kite and challenged a gun crew to use it as a target, which was more realistic than shooting at clouds. To the crew's exasperation, they had to fire many rounds before making a direct hit. The captain of the ship was so impressed with the demonstration that he ordered Garber to build more target kites.

As the gunners improved their shooting accuracy, Garber modified an Eddy kite that could swing across the sky, loop, dive, do figure eights, and climb along two lines. The kite was controlled by a flier with a twin-spool reel complete with control bar and brake. A ventral fin and rudder on the kite aided in directional control. A silhouette of a Japanese Zero or German Focke-Wulf-190 plane was silkscreened on a light blue rayon sail. At a distance the blue background disappeared, revealing only the kite's silhouette of an aircraft. Eventually the wooden struts of the target kites were replaced with aluminum so that they would sink after being shot down.

■ **BELOW, LEFT:** Buck Rogers "Jet-Propelled" strato-kite, "The Kite that Flies Like an Aeroplane," ca. 1946.

■ **ABOVE:** Gibson-Girl box kite being launched by "downed" airmen during World War II.

The Garber target kite was credited with saving an aircraft carrier. One morning the gunners were stationed in their bays for target practice when a lookout sighted a Japanese torpedo plane approaching from a bank of clouds. Had they not been ready and called to general quarters, the plane would have seriously damaged the carrier. Instead the gunners were able to down the enemy plane.

During the war some 300,000 target kites were produced by A. G. Spalding and Brothers. Both the U.S. and British armies adopted these target kites. After the war a few target kites surfaced in military surplus stores; today they are a rare collector's item.

Garber also used winged, triangular box (signal) kites to pass important papers from ship to aircraft. A cable with the package attached was strung between two kites. A passing aircraft would snare the cable with a hook and deliver the package to its destination.

In 1948, Francis Rogallo introduced the first modern kite. Rogallo, an engineer, theorized that a flexible wing would conform to the airflow and be more stable than a rigid wing. He carried out his experiments using a piece of curtain and a fan. The result was a flexible, parawing kite. His concept was studied by engineers in the United States as a means of landing returning space capsules. Today the parawing is best known as a prototype for the modern hang glider.

Rogallo's kite also led to the development of the keeled delta-wing kite by Gayla Industries (patented in 1958) and Al (the "Nantucket kiteman") Hartig (patented in 1967). The delta proved to have slightly different flight characteristics, being able to soar as well as adjust to the ever-changing wind.

North Pacific Productions manufactured a very successful commercial parawing kite called a "Glite." In 1964, the Glite was promoted as a kite that could be flown on a single or dual line, making it the first kite sold for aerobatics (stunting).

Another twentieth-century kite design was the sled kite, which was patented by William Allison in 1950. The Allison sled is a close kin to Rogallo's Flexi-kite because there are no lateral supports. Both rely on the wind to keep them open and flying. The sled version best known today was popularized by Frank Scott in 1964. The Scott sled kite has parallel struts and is vented for stability; the original ventless sled had three vertical struts supporting a tapered sail. Today, there is also a ram-air sled that has evolved from Jalbert's parafoil.

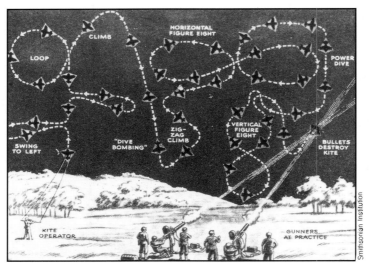

■ **ABOVE, TOP:** Preparing to launch a Garber target kite, World War II.

■ **ABOVE:** Francis Rogallo with his flexi-kite (Nags Head, North Carolina).

■ **ABOVE, RIGHT:** Poster showing a target kite maneuver, World War II.

■ **OPPOSITE PAGE:** Commander Paul Garber with a target kite displaying a silhouette of a Japanese Zero.

Domina Jalbert's parafoil kite was a breakthrough development. Jalbert worked with balloons and kites during World War II to create his tethered parafoil kite in 1964. Today this kite is best known as the prototype for the rectangular parachute used by sky divers. Jalbert has dedicated his life to harnessing the wind with balloons, sails, kites, and parachutes. Until his death in 1991, Jalbert could be found in his "aerology" laboratory developing new "wind harnessing" inventions.

The kite that can claim the biggest impact on modern kiting was the dual-line "stunter" by the Englishman Peter Powell in 1972. In the sixties, Powell used several lines to help solve a balancing problem in a single-line kite. He found that with the extra lines it was possible to steer and control the kite. A decade passed before he could perfect his stunter. He gained fame in 1975 when he was awarded the silver diploma for his kite at the Exhibition of New Inventions and Techniques in Geneva.

Powell gained further publicity in 1976 when he won the British "Toy of the Year" award.

The stunter kite's real claim to fame is not that it is the first aerobatics kite but the first to be accepted as an adult's kite, not a child's toy. The stunter kite is capable of being flown in a wide range of winds, and several can be tied one behind the other for additional variety. A long tube tail follows through each maneuver to echo the movement. Powell's stunter kite led to the public's awareness of kiting as a sport and not just child's play.

Over the last decade there have been many advances in kite design, as well as an increase in the popularity of kite flying. The introduction of synthetic materials such as polyethylene, nylon, carbon rod, and fiberglass have aided in this development. Kite flying has been raised from the status of "kid's stuff" to that of a recreational sport and recognized art form. Some kites, such as those from Japan, have become valuable collector's items.

© Andre Baget

■ **OPPOSITE PAGE:** Gibson-Girl box kite (with generator) and Garber target kite from the author's collection.

■ **ABOVE:** Matin Lester's "running legs" parafoil.

■ **LEFT:** Stack of three Peter Powell stunt kites.

© Christopher Bain

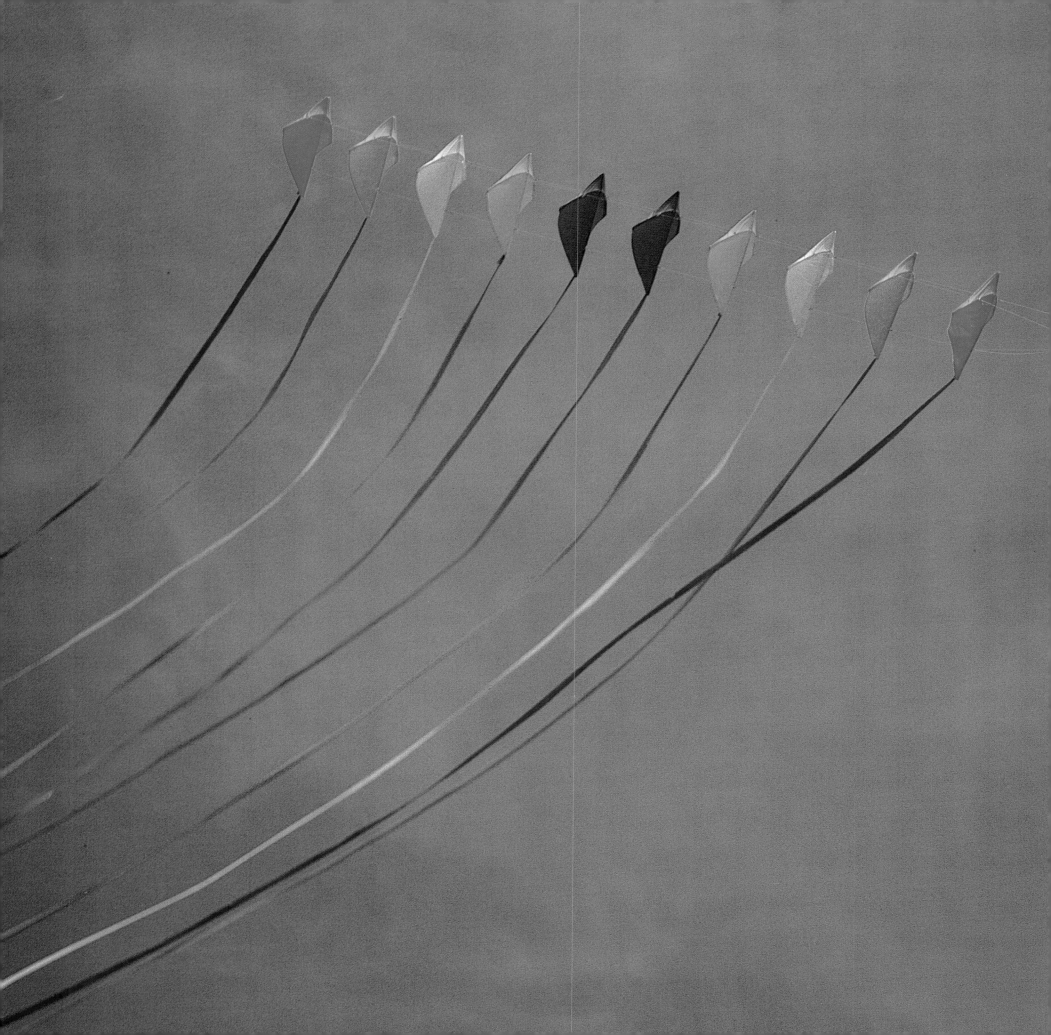

CHAPTER TWO

◆

Choosing
a Kite

■ **RIGHT, BELOW:** Child's Delta with animal appliqué.

■ **OPPOSITE PAGE:** Dale Kitchens launches his 1.5 Malay, as seen through a Delta-Conyne.

I often meet people who are intimidated by the art of kite flying. They blame themselves for not being able to make their kites fly when it is more than likely that the fault lies in the kite design. The biggest offender is the traditional diamond kite. Unless special aerodynamic principles are considered, the diamond kite's shape makes for an unstable flier. Just because you purchased your kite from a store, there is no guarantee that the kite will fly well. Many kites need a slight adjustment to match the weather conditions. Others are so poorly designed that they will never fly. A kite's flight is

© Francis Hall/Kite Post

affected by the type of materials, bridle length, tow point, tail length or type, balance, flying location, and even by weather conditions.

Like most children, I made kites as a boy. My creations didn't fly well, but the fun was just making a kite. About twenty years ago I seriously tried making kites to sell at a fair. It was very frustrating because none of the kites flew! Instead of giving up, I used the basic shapes, changed materials, and successfully built my designs. I always carry extra tail material in my box of tricks to solve stability problems. One rule of thumb is that if a kite is built so strong that it will not break, then it is more than likely too heavy to fly.

Another lesson I soon learned was that different kite designs don't act the same way; there is no "all-round kite." Each style has a different function and appeal to the flier. Not everyone can sit and watch a kite just dance around up in the sky. For these people there are fighter or stunt kites that can be steered about the sky for extra enjoyment. The box kite is a popular choice for "engineer" types who are fascinated by how this kite flies. On the other hand, an "artist" might like the grace of a delta, the slow roll of a hexagonal kite, or the geometric patterns of a multifaceted kite.

Generally kites can be classed as either stable or maneuverable. A stable flier is the type of kite that flies itself: They include deltas, dragons, parafoils, and box kites. The maneuverable kite category sometimes falls under the heading of sport kites: They are the action kites such as star tumblers, stunters, and fighter kites.

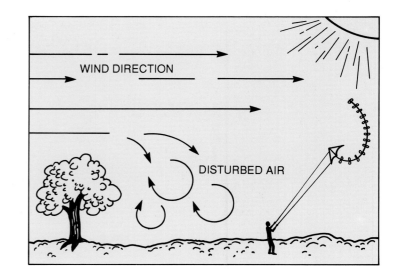

Wind Scale

Before you begin kite flying, the first thing that you should consider is the type of wind in your area. It doesn't matter how much you run if the wind is not strong enough to support a kite's weight—it just will not fly. For example, a box kite can be flown in strong winds, while a delta is better suited for less windy conditions. I usually have several different kites to fly to match changing wind conditions. Remember that in some areas the wind can change dramatically in a few hours.

Keep the following wind speeds in mind as a rough estimate.

© Francis Hall/Kite Post

CALM (2–3 mph [3–5 kph])—Smoke drifts slowly and flags show little movement—very difficult to fly a kite.

LIGHT (4–7 mph [6–11 kph])—Leaves rustle and flags flutter—light kites fly (e.g., ultra-light stunter, fighter, and delta kites).

GENTLE (8–12 mph [12–19 kph])—Leaves rustle and flags fly—most kites fly.

MODERATE (13–18 mph [20–29 kph])—Trees toss and dust flies—any kite will fly. Wear gloves to fly big kites.

FRESH (19–24 mph [30–39 kph])—Small trees sway—sometimes called "kite weather"—fly box or stunt kites.

STRONG (25–31 mph [40–49 kph])—Large branches sway—kite line breaks and flying kites can be risky—fly only box or stunt kites, or stay home and build a kite.

Remember to stay downwind of trees, buildings, and hills, since the wind gets disturbed by such vertical obstructions. The rule of thumb is a simple 1:5 ratio: If a tree is 30 feet (9 m) tall, stay at least 150 (45 m) downwind of it to allow the wind to stop swirling. Many people are frustrated in their early attempts at kite-flying simply because they didn't seek out an open flying field, but instead chose a field surrounded by tall trees.

■ **LEFT:** Launching a multi-celled tetrahedral kite.

■ **OPPOSITE PAGE, ABOVE:** Delta-Conyne. This kite has the lift of a delta and the stability of a box kite.

■ **OPPOSITE PAGE, BELOW:** On the end of a line, a winged-star box kite becomes a kinetic sculpture.

Kite Materials

The types of materials used in kites are limited only by one's imagination, skill, money, and the wind available to lift the kite. It is helpful to know that heavy materials tend to cause a kite to spin more than lighter types. Someone once said that even a barn door will fly in a gale—the problem is where to attach the flying line. In the Pacific, islanders have made their kites from leaves for centuries. In Houston, Texas, the late John Jordan, an eccentric kite flyer who wrote a book about his unique kite creations, *Make Your Own Kite*, used junk for his unusual kites. I like my students to make simple kites out of folded paper as an introduction to kite making. You may be surprised to see how many adults can hardly believe that a piece of typing paper can fly.

Sail

Today the traditional paper kite is rarely seen in the West because it will not withstand rough treatment. In the Orient kites are not meant to last beyond the festival where they are flown. For example, in the small fishing village of Sagara, Japan, teams practice a 300-year-old kite-fighting festival. Traditionally, each kite is destroyed either in battle or after the event so that its "soul" can be released to be reborn in the following year's kites.

Many Malaysian and Indian kites are covered with a glazed, waterproof tissue paper to withstand high humidity, but they still tear very easily. By far the strongest and most expensive paper is Japanese *washi*, which is handmade mulberry paper, not to be confused with rice paper. For very large kites the Japanese use either very heavy, layered, or silk-covered *washi*. On a very windy day in southern Japan, I once saw a modern Western kite break up under the pressure of strong winds while the Japanese paper kites flew intact.

Most commercial kites are made from either synthetic cloth or plastic. A very popular cloth is a lightweight, "ripstop" nylon that is used for spinnakers on sailing boats. It is a sturdy material that has been urethane-coated to make it windproof. The other types of ripstop that are used in hot-air balloons, outdoor wear, and tents tend to stretch too much for most kites.

■ **ABOVE, TOP:** Sagara Dako made from handmade paper (washi). It was traditional in the fishing village of Sagara, Japan, that kites surviving the kite festival (battle) were destroyed. It was thought that the soul would be released and reborn in the following year's kites.

■ **ABOVE:** Close-up of a ripstop nylon, cellular kite. In the West, kites are mainly built to last.

■ **OPPOSITE PAGE:** A Rantan Dako by Kazuho Inoue (Nagoya, Japan) looks as beautiful hanging in an art museum as it does in the sky.

OPPOSITE PAGE: This Edo Kaku Dako (Tokyo, Japan) is made from silk covered washi. The rabbit and wave theme was probably taken from an old folk belief that a female rabbit conceives by dancing across the waves on the eighteenth day of the eighth moon.

LEFT: Soburo Imai painting a Shirone Kaku Ika. The painting is of Ishikawa Goemen who was glorified as a "Robin Hood" in the Kabuki play, "Sanmon Gosan-no-kiri."

Plastic kites are generally made from a low- or high-density polyethylene. Their durability is usually reflected in the plastic's weight or the kite's sturdy construction. Generally, plastic kites are mass-produced, inexpensive, and fairly decent fliers. Mylar, a polyester film, is another popular plastic kite material. It is very strong for its weight, but once punctured it will easily tear. In the seventies, metallic mylar dragon kites were very popular but were withdrawn from the market when it was discovered that they can conduct electricity. Another plastic that has been used in kite making is Tyvek, a spun-bonded polyethylene made by DuPont. It is available in various weights in either a cloth or a paper-parchment form. The main drawback with Tyvek is that it is only manufactured in white and doesn't dye well. Tyvek can be sewn, glued, and painted and printed on.

Frame (Struts)

Wood is the least expensive strut material used in the West. By far the most popular is the all-round hardwood dowel available at any hardware store. When compared to other materials, dowels are the least resilient, being subject to breakage and defects. Their advantages are cost, availability, and ease of repair. Today flat sticks, traditionally used in American kites (some split from sides of orange crates), are rarely used in commercial kites.

Asians traditionally made their struts from bamboo ("nature's fiberglass"). This material is still used today because of its availability and high strength-to-weight ratio. Some bamboo struts are tapered or bent to allow the kite to flex in a set fashion. A strut's strength is determined by the type and the part of the bamboo used.

Solid fiberglass rod is gaining popularity in the West for smaller kites. It is almost indestructible but heavier and more flexible than other materials. Where flexibility is a concern, fiberglass tubing (filament-wound epoxy) is often used (e.g., stunt kites). It is a moderately heavy, rigid, and durable material, but expensive.

An even more costly and lighter strut material, now gaining popularity with stunt fliers, is extruded or wrapped graphite tubing. The top of the line for stiffness and durability (among the most expensive) is a carbon fiber–aluminum composite made by Easton. This material is often used in ultralight stunter kites. In the past there was some controversy over the use of carbon rod or metal in kites because they could conduct electricity.

© Wayne Hosking

© Mike Wilmer

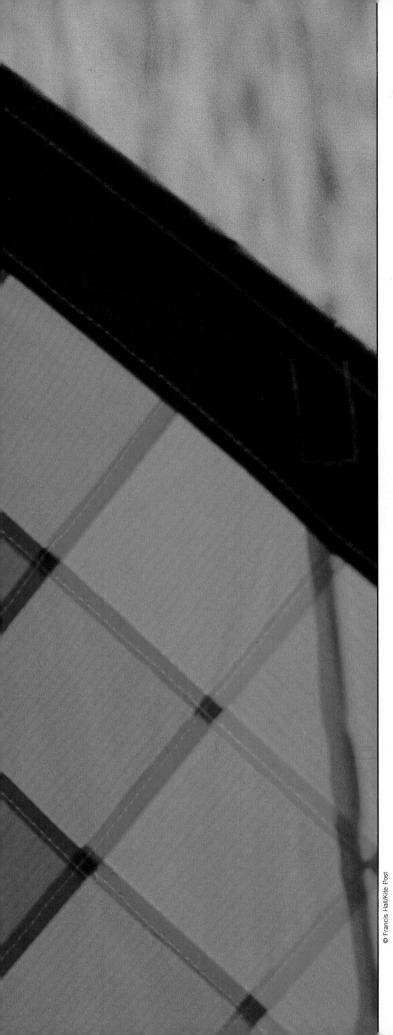

© Francis Hall/Kite Post

© Wayne Hosking

■ **OPPOSITE PAGE:** A close-up of a colorful ripstop nylon kite showing a stained glass effect. If the pattern is too small this effect will be lost in the sky.

■ **LEFT:** Making *washi*.

■ **BELOW:** The Tunezumi family making Sode Dako (sleeve kites).

© Wayne Hosking

CHAPTER THREE

◆

Single-Line Kites

© Francis Hall/Kite Post

© Christopher Bain

The best way to introduce yourself to kite flying is to find a medium-sized kite and some line and start flying it as soon as you feel the urge to go outside and enjoy a sunny day. Try to choose a kite that best suits the wind conditions. Ask at your local kite store or send for one of the many mail-order catalogs for more information on kites. Read a few of the major kite magazines. It is also advisable to keep clear of more exotic types of kites until you have experienced a few outings. There is literally a whole world of kites for you to choose from.

© Andre Baget

■ Groger's hybrid parasled flies almost effortlessly toward the sky.

Kite Varieties

DIAMOND AND OTHER FLAT KITES. The traditional flat diamond kite (two sticks) with the long tail has lost popularity with the introduction of more modern and more efficient kites. This is the kite that has caused many people to give up on them. They blame themselves when the kite will not fly. Today many of the appliqué diamond kites sold in stores are best suited for wall hangings.

The barn door ("American three-sticker"), America's first indigenous kite, is a strong-pulling kite. Other flat, three-stick kites include the Bermudian three-stick and hexagonal kites. Like the flat diamond kites, they fly at a low angle and require long tails for stability. They are best left to intermediate fliers.

EDDY DIAMOND AND OTHER BOWED KITES. A true Eddy is a tailless diamond kite that is as wide as it is tall, with the cross strut one-fifth down the spine. The cross strut is bowed (or set) to form a dihedral, which generally stabilizes the kite without the use of a long tail (or any tail). Some commercial diamond kites have thin bowed cross struts that bend back in the wind (like the cross struts on fighting kites), creating a dihedral. If you are going to fly a diamond kite, fly one that has a bow, either in the wind or by some other device.

One of the most popular kites from Japan is the tailless *rokkaku*, which is a six-sided kite with two bowed cross struts and a removable spine. (Most Japanese kites are flown bowed and tailless.) The Western ripstop version will fly just as well as a delta kite.

DRAGON KITES. These kites may have originated from the paper Thai serpent kite. They have broad heads and long tapered tails. Except for the long tail the dragon is not regarded as a large kite. They are usually made from nylon, ripstop, or Mylar and require a steady breeze to fly. In the right conditions they make an excellent beginner's kite. The octopus, a variant of the dragon, with its large head and short multiple tails, makes an excellent children's kite.

SLED KITES. This type of kite is made up of a sail supported by two or more vertical struts. The pressure of the wind holds the kite open. This is a unique kite because it has keels and a bridle. The sled is a simple kite that is as close to an all-round kite for the beginner that I have found. There are many variations of the sled with the vented Scott sled gaining the most coverage. Sometimes vents cause sled kites to collapse in the wind; the ventless versions are often more stable.

The parasled, or pocket kite, is a strutless sled kite that uses inflated tubes instead of sticks for support. This is a very handy kite to carry in your pocket, backpack, boat, or car, while you are traveling. I found them to be excellent as gifts to give during my travels to Asia.

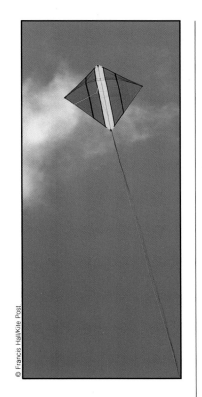

■ **ABOVE:** A ripstop nylon fighter kite. Although it is usually flown tailless, a tail can be added for extra stability.

■ **BELOW, LEFT:** A ripstop nylon version of the popular Japanese *rokkaku*, custom designed in the shape of a turtle.

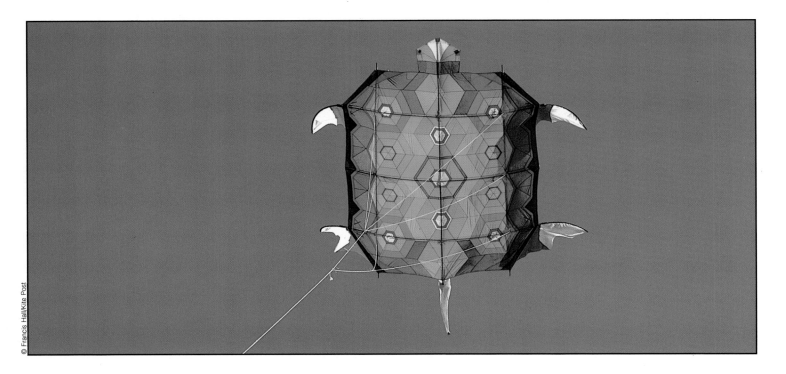

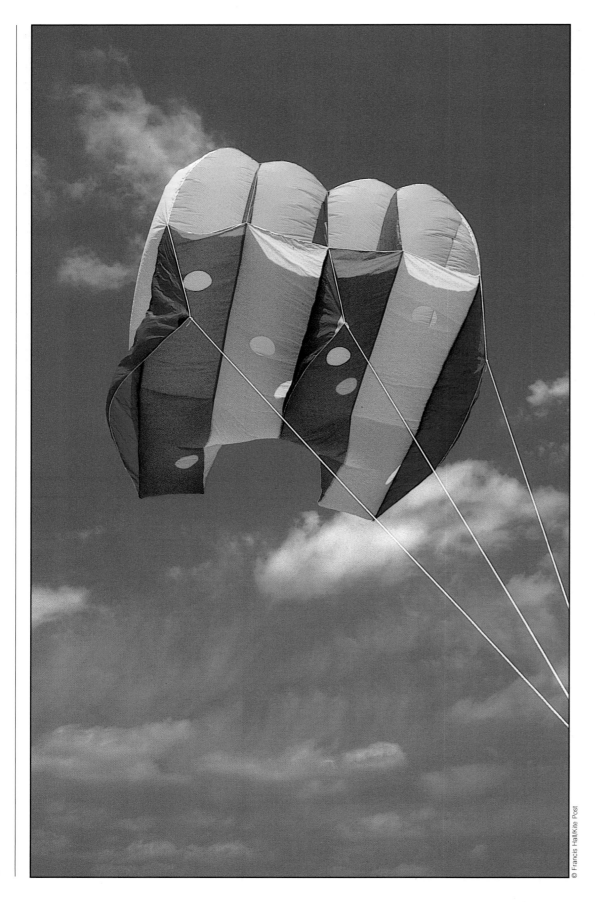

PARAFOILS. This tethered airfoil is a cross between a balloon, an airplane wing, a parachute, and a kite. It doesn't have any sticks and relies on a series of air chambers that are inflated by the wind. A series of triangular ventrals, or keels, gives it lateral stability. The parafoil is one of the most efficient lifting devices yet devised. Many fliers use parafoils to carry wind socks and spinners for an extra impact. Because of its pull, flying a large parafoil can be very dangerous for the novice. Other parafoil variants include the Stratascoop, Paraflate, and Flowform.

DELTA-WING KITES. These are triangular-shaped, single-plane, tailless kites with a keel, instead of a bridle, for stability. They are easy to fly and are an excellent beginner's kite. Every flier should have at least one in his or her kite bag.

Medium to large ripstop nylon deltas will often fly in light wind conditions and soar well on moderate breezes. They don't handle turbulence very well and will tend to pull to one side or even "candle down" in unstable wind. Some small commercial plastic kites are poorly designed and will not fly well without a tail. (These kites, however, are generally the exception rather than the rule.)

BOX KITES. These include a broad category of tailless, cellular kites. Since their invention by Lawrence Hargrave at the end of the last century, they have been regarded as the "workhorse of kites." This reputation comes from the fact that the box configuration makes for a very efficient, high-angle flier that develops substantial lift.

The basic box kite has two cells supported by four side and four removable, internal cross struts. Because of its structure, the box kite needs a moderate to strong wind to fly. In other words, when people say that it is "kite weather," it is time to reach for a box kite. The addition of wings creates more lift, which allows a box kite to be flown in less windy conditions. Though this kite is an excellent flier, a beginner should take into account the strong pull when selecting the size of a box kite to purchase.

The rhombus box is a box kite that has been flattened so it has more lifting surface into the wind. This allows it to be flown in lighter wind conditions but with the loss of some stability in strong breezes.

The Cody box kite is a Hargrave box with curved wings, which makes for a high-performance flier. The wings give the kite extra lift, and they can be tied one behind the other.

© Andre Baget

© Francis Hall/Kite Post

■ **ABOVE:** Dan Leigh's six-winged box.

■ **LEFT:** Early Cody compound box kite.

■ **OPPOSITE PAGE:** Sutton flowform.

The French military or Conyne box kite is a winged triangular-shaped box kite that is best known for lifting military observers. It is a favorite with beginners and experienced fliers.

The Delta-Conyne kite is a compound kite with the efficiency of a delta and the stability of a triangular box. They are high-angle fliers that stay aloft well on unstable winds—a favorite with beginner and experienced fliers.

Peter Lynn's Tri-D is a winged box kite with each lifting surface a triangle, making it an excellent flier in light to moderate winds.

Professor Waldof's box kite has set the trend for many of today's compound box kites, which are regarded as being flying sculptures. These kites have multiple wings and sails, and as they fly their form changes in the wind.

Tumbling stars are multiwinged compound box kites that are fun to fly. They are as stable as any other box kite on a steady line. Release the line and it will spin and tumble until the flier takes up the slack again. On a steady line the star will recover and climb high in the sky.

Facet kites are multicell kites with a central spine and external supports. They often go by the names of snowflake or reflex kites, and they are very stable fliers in a wide range of wind conditions with little pull.

Tetrahedral kites are made up of triangular pyramids with each cell having two lifting surfaces supported by six struts. They tend to be heavy and require a strong wind to fly. The tetrahedral holds a fascination for many fliers but is best left to the experienced flier.

ROTOR OR REVOLVING-WING KITES. These kites are generally rotating airfoils or gyrocoptic kites that create lift through their rotating motion. They usually are only fair fliers and have mainly been marketed as novelties or children's toys.

FIGHTER KITES. Kite fighting has been a sport in Asia for centuries, and kites still play a special part in many festivals. Traditionally, fighters are highly balanced, lightweight kites made from paper and bamboo. They are usually small, tailless, and very agile, requiring special skills to make and fly. Each country or region has developed its own fighting style and technique. Countries known for kite fighting include the Philippines, Thailand, China, Hong Kong, Malaysia, Indonesia, Japan, Korea, India, Pakistan, Brazil, Chile, and the West Indies.

Fighters are single-line stunt kites that are controlled by increasing or decreasing tension on the line. With a slack line the kite is flat and will tend to spin. Apply pressure to the line, and the kite will become three-

■ Train of Delta-Conyne kites.

■ **OPPOSITE PAGE:** Dragon Kite, Aso Kite Festival (Mt. Aso, Japan).

dimensional and travel in the direction that it is pointing. To change the direction, release tension on the line; the kite will stop and start to turn. With practice you can continuously spin most kites by quickly feeding out line when they begin to turn.

The object of a kite fight is to outmaneuver an opponent and to cut the line of the other kite with a specially prepared line. The other flier in turn either attacks or retreats until one of the lines is cut. A defense strategy is to quickly let out line so that one line slides harmlessly across another. A taut line is easier to cut than a slack line.

Not all single-line flyers are bent on destruction. The attraction for many Westerners is not the actual "fighting" but the challenge between the flier, kite, and wind. You steer the kite through your fingertips, with a delicate control and a feeling of oneness with the kite. It is very easy to become engrossed with kite flying and oblivious to the rest of the world. One might even say kite flying is a form of Zen meditation. An Indian once expressed the experience as "having one's heart out on the string" and "a way to kiss the sky."

The wind in the United States tends to be too strong for the imported Indian fighter's frail, tissue paper sails. Today there is a new breed of "fighter" available at kite stores or by mail order. They can also be called single-line stunt kites or even kinetic art. Made of sturdy modern materials, they will withstand the punishment of strong winds and errors in flying technique. With more people being exposed to the peace and pure pleasure of kite fighting and flirting with the wind, the sport is undergoing a renaissance.

ORIENTAL KITES. The common denominator of Oriental kites is that they are made of bamboo and paper. An exception would be the silk or synthetic kites from China. Their shape and purpose (some are made in accordance with an established ceremony) are as varied as the stars in the sky. A plain, undecorated Oriental kite is unthinkable, and most are sold in this country as wall hangings.

They are generally well constructed, being made by skilled craftsmen. Some require an experienced hand to fly, since they can be difficult to control, but an extra tail can often solve this problem. You should be aware that some exotic kites, like the Malaysian *wau,* take great skill to fly and plenty of air space. They are designed to make large arcs in the sky to create noise from the hummer.

Do not expect a paper kite to last more than a kite season or even one day's outing. An exception is the

© Wayne Hosking

sturdy Japanese kites made from *washi* (handmade mulberry paper).

SPECIALTY KITES. There are many new kites now available that don't fit into an established category. You can find kites shaped like birds, planes, boats, trains, and even flying castles. Most are very specialized and take some understanding of kite flying to master. Giant kites and artistic versions (kinetic sculptures) of standard kites can also be a handful for the novice.

■ **OPPOSITE PAGE:** Randy Tom's Patrick Nagel Seven-sisters kite.

■ **ABOVE:** Bobby Stanfield's "Pro Spirit" kite.

■ **LEFT:** Rick Cole's remake of Ohasi's Expansible box kite.

63

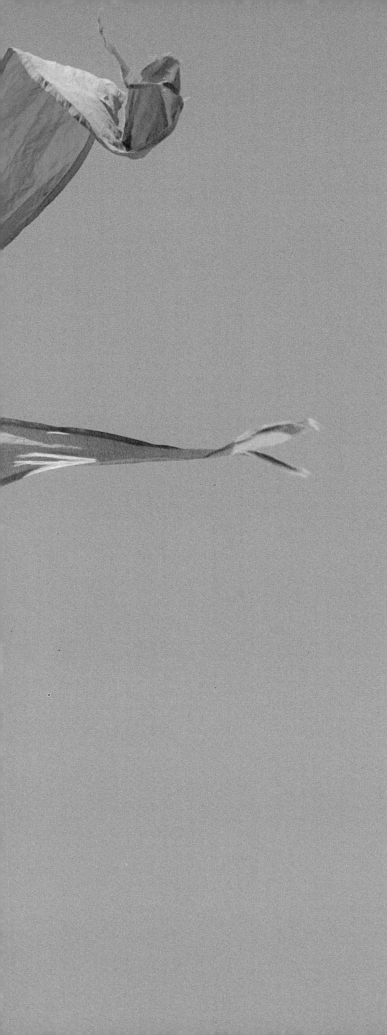

Single-Line Accessories

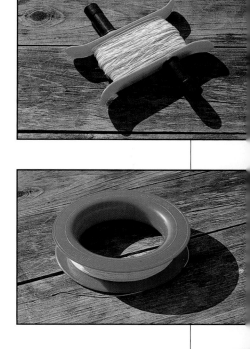

LINES. Your choice of line will be dictated by your kite, and the line type will often influence how your kite flies. A heavy line will tend to pull a kite downward; a light line has the risk of snapping. The traditional cotton flying line tends to be so "fuzzy" that it catches the wind and pulls a kite off balance. The most common lines used by kite fliers are either twisted or braided nylon or polyester. Small fighting kites should be flown on lightweight line that doesn't stretch very much, like cotton, polyester, or linen thread. I often use dental floss or buttonhole thread for my smaller kites, including fighter kites.

When buying line, make sure you know your kite's size, type, and pull. A line's tensile strength doesn't indicate the load that the line will carry or the kite's pull. For safety the line–to–load ratio should be about 6:1 (e.g., 30-pound [11-kg] test line will safely fly a kite with a 5-pound [2-kg] pull). A rule of thumb when calculating the strength of line to use is to multiply the area of the kite in square feet (sq m) by three. For example, a kite 3 by 3 feet (.9 m by .9 m) has an area of 9 square feet (.8 sq m) and can be safely flown on a 30-pound (11-kg) test line.

There are several types of line that should be avoided. Monofilament fishing line is difficult to see and so can be a hazard on the flying field. But by far the most dangerous is wire. It has been the cause of injury or death to many kite fliers over the last century. You should not be fooled by plastic-coated or sleeved wire—if the wire crosses a power line, you will end your kite-flying days.

SPOOLS, BOBBINS, HANDLES, WINDERS, AND REELS. These accessories are all used to store flying line. Always use a line holder that allows for quick retrieval and release of line without creating tangles. There is a large variety to choose from, with a large price range to match. Expect to pay less for a simple plastic spool and more for a custom wooden reel. Some fliers like to use fishing rods.

CARRYING BAGS. These are convenient for carrying and storing kites. Many have accessory pockets for kite line and sundry items. They are fairly inexpensive. The hard-sided, telescopic fishing rod tubes make secure traveling cases.

WIND GAUGE. This can give you a visual aid in determining the wind at the flying field. The major drawback is that you will be observing ground wind speeds only.

■ **OPPOSITE PAGE:** Large windsock.

■ **ABOVE, TOP TO BOTTOM:** Carey winder, Halo spool, Wooden spool.

© Christopher Bain

© Christopher Bain (all)

65

■ **RIGHT:** Double Delta-Conyne with spinning windsocks attached to its line.

■ **BELOW, RIGHT:** Winslow Colwell uses gloves to fly his large *rokkaku* kites.

GLOVES. Gloves are advisable for strong-pulling kites. I buy gloves in hardware stores; the more expensive types (without fingers) are found in sporting goods stores.

WIND SOCKS AND SPINNERS. These can be attached to a kite or line. In some spectacular aerial displays they are referred to as "sky junk." Their size dictates their cost. Before hanging anything on your kite, make sure that it can handle the load and drag.

DOG SPIKE (KITE ANCHOR). This is handy to tie off a kite for hands-free flying, when there is nothing else in the area. For safety's sake, a kite shouldn't be left flying unattended. Kite anchors are available at pet and kite stores.

STROBES, MICRO LIGHTS, OR LIGHT STICKS. These aids are used for night flying. They will add a new dimension to kite-flying fun.

Flying a Kite

Now that you have a kite, you are probably itching to go out and fly it. The first thing to check is if the wind conditions are either too light or too strong for your kite. When tree branches are tossing about, many people mistakenly call it "kite weather." The best kites in these conditions would be box or stunt kites. Other kites might fly, but you will risk damaging or even losing them. If there is a thunderstorm in your area, leave your kite at home, since kite lines will conduct electricity. Of course, this was proven by Ben Franklin's very dangerous experiment.

Next, find a flying area. The best places to fly are in open areas far away from power lines, trees, buildings, roadways, and airports. Avoid flying a kite downwind of tall objects. I usually look for a beach, park, or open field, keeping in mind that trees, buildings, or terrain may spoil the wind quality, creating what is known as a "wind shadow." To the inexperienced flier, the wind may feel like it is blowing in one direction, but it may actually be rolling and flowing around objects, creating ground turbulence that makes kite flying difficult. Generally speaking, an object that is 100 feet (30 m) tall will create a wind shadow of 500 feet (150 m) In an unknown area I watch the action and direction of flags, trees, or smoke for an indicator that there is a wind disturbance.

If you are alone, let out some line and, with your back to the wind, raise the kite upward. Hold the kite away from you so as not to block the wind. When the wind catches the kite, slowly pump on the line. Do not pull too hard, because this will often cause the kite to dive. Just keep pumping and feeding out line until the kite reaches the desired altitude. Don't let the line run through your fingers rapidly, or you may receive a burn or cut.

If your kite spins or dives, release tension on the line so that the kite can right itself or land safely. Pulling hard on the line will only increase the speed of the dive or spin. Check to see if your kite has enough of a tail, that the bridle is not hung up, or that the kite is balanced. With a delta kite, check to see that the side struts are all the way back in their sleeves.

If your kite refuses to fly, first check to see if the wind conditions are suitable, whether there is too much tail, or if the tow point is in the correct position.

Sometimes the ground level winds are light, while higher up they are stronger. Observe smoke rising, flags, or leaves on tall trees to indicate this situation. Another problem might be that the lower winds are turbulent because of trees or buildings. The best solution to these problems is to have an assistant help with a "high launch." Your assistant should be downwind 50 to 100 feet (15 to 30 m), holding the kite with the flying line taut. On a given signal the assistant launches the kite with a slight upward push. As the kite rises, pump and release more line.

Flying a Fighter

Fighting kites are inherently unstable in the air. This is especially true near the ground level where there is usually air turbulence. The beginner should have an assistant for a "high launch." Once in the sky, fighter kites require fingertip control. The addition of a tail will help stabilize the kite until you have a better feel for it.

Small, sharp jabs on the line to pull in or release tension will usually cause the kite to turn. When the kite is facing the required direction, pull hard on the line; the kite will travel in that direction. To stop a dive, release tension on the line; the kite will stop and start to spin again. A kite positioned to your left will tend to spin to the right; a kite to the right will tend to spin to the left. With a little practice, the fighter kite can be maneuvered about the sky at will.

It is very bad etiquette to try to engage anyone in a kite fight who doesn't want to fight. This is especially true if the other person is flying a regular single-line kite.

■ Bill Lockhart's "quilted" *rokkaku*.

CHAPTER FOUR

Stunt Kites

■ **RIGHT:** Top of the Line's newest swept wing stunter, the North Shore Radical.

■ **OPPOSITE PAGE:** Stack of Shadow stunters at field no. 6 (Jones Beach, New York).

A stunter is a steerable kite capable of doing loops, swoops, and dives with the pilot in full control. Normally two lines are used to control the flight. A stunter can be flown with or without a tail. A long tail adds extra movement to the maneuvers but also extra drag that will slow down a kite.

Over the last two decades there have been several attempts to market a commercial aerobatics kite. None had universal acceptance until 1972 when Peter Powell introduced his dual-line diamond stunter. The Powell Skymaster was made from heavy-gauge plastic

■ The illustration shows three team flyers practicing a basic figure eight in a follow-the-leader exercise. The flying lines need to be different lengths to avoid midair collisions. Usually the lead flyer's lines are 5 feet (1.5 m) longer than flyer #2, whose lines are 5 feet (1.5 m) longer than flyer #3, and so on. Flyers with the same length lines often stagger their body positions relative to each other to create the needed difference in lengths.

■ **BELOW:** Force 10 stunter with a massive 16-foot (5-m) wing span.

■ **BELOW RIGHT:** The Flash Angel from Rare Air in England soars above the surf.

■ **OPPOSITE PAGE:** Stack of Peter Powell Stunters at Liberty State Park, New Jersey. The Statue of Liberty can be seen in the background.

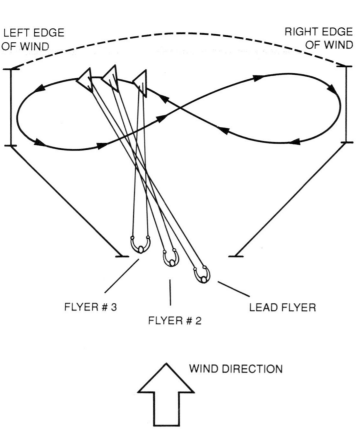

LEFT EDGE OF WIND

RIGHT EDGE OF WIND

FLYER # 3

FLYER # 2

LEAD FLYER

WIND DIRECTION

with aluminum alloy struts. A spring wire fitting in the kite's front allowed it to adjust to different wind conditions. Today the Powell stunter has a fiberglass frame with either a plastic or a ripstop nylon sail.

Powell's success attracted many competitors. With the introduction of more efficient kites such as the foil (Flexifoil—1976), small diamond "stacks" (Rainbows—1977), delta Rogallo wing (Skynasaur—1978), small delta "stacks" (Hyperkites—1980), swept wings (Phoenix 20—1982, Action 8.2—1983, Hawaiian team kite—1984), and quad line (Revolution—1988), stunt flying has grown in

popularity. Today, stunt competitions are held internationally and attract the top fliers around the world.

There are approximately 150 different models of stunt kites on the market today. The popularity of sport kites has resulted in new stunters being introduced each month. Many of them don't gain a foothold in the market and don't last long.

You should select a kite that best suits your budget, flying ability, and wind conditions. Stunt kites can be purchased from around fifteen dollars, advancing up to a custom kite that can cost more than five hundred dollars. A complete outfit consisting of kite, line, and accessories will generally cost between one and three hundred dollars. People who are shocked by the high cost of stunt kites should compare them to other high-quality sporting equipment. Inexpensive two-line kites are available, but they don't perform—nor do they last—to the level of a competition-grade stunt kite.

Stunt kites are still evolving, and there are no official standards to test one kite against another. Because there are so many kites to choose from, you will have to rely on

© Andre Baget

© Joe Gschwind

the advice of retailers or friends or read magazine re-
views. You should consider that some recommendations
will be biased. My stunt kite can perform just as well as
many high-performance ripstop and fiberglass kites. The
best method is to fly as many kites as you can get your
hands on and compare them firsthand.

Stunters are available to fly in a variety of wind
speeds. A kite that is designed to fly in a light breeze
may prove too fragile for strong wind; a kite for heavy
winds will not launch in light conditions. The delta and
foil designs are able to fly in lighter winds and a wider
range of conditions because of their superior lift and
aerodynamic structure. You should know the prevailing
wind conditions in your area and the kites' recommended wind ranges before making a choice. Many fliers
carry a bag of kites and lines to suit all conditions.

Any variation in sail material (ripstop nylon, plastic, or
Dacron) or struts (fiberglass, graphite, or wood) can
affect a kite's performance. You also should be aware
that slight variations in adjustment or construction can
cause different flight characteristics in kites of the same
design. Even different wind conditions can cause a kite
to react differently. This is especially true with swept-
wing stunters. It is advisable to learn how to "tune" your
kite to suit various conditions.

If you are a novice, you may consider starting with a
basic stunter (e.g., a Powell, Dyna-kite, or Trlby kite) to
get the feel of stunt flying. If you are not sure of your
abilities, try to find someone who will give you lessons.
Diamond stunters are generally less expensive than deltas or foils because of their simpler construction. The
former also tend to fly more slowly and are more durable, which make them excellent for beginners.

It is possible to start with an advanced-level kite that
offers more opportunities to make flying very exciting.
Some people will have little problem, while others will
risk damaging their kite before learning how to fly it
correctly. For ease of control, it is best to begin with a
three-quarter-sized kite. Most kites are built sturdy
enough to withstand the novice flier (or they can be
repaired). Depending on your abilities, it can take between twenty minutes and many weeks to master a
stunter.

For children, you should consider stunt kites that have
less pull and more control. And you should also remember that they will be flying a kite that can reach speeds in
excess of 60 miles per hour (97 kph) and can injure
bystanders or themselves.

Diamond and Rogallo Wing Kites

Paul Garber's World War II target kite was a modified Eddy diamond. Garber added a steering rudder to his kite for extra control. Today many toy kite manufacturers have added two lines to their diamond kites and called them stunt kites. These kites can be described at best as steerable kites because they are inefficient stunters that fly in a narrow wind range. I prefer to call them "toys." The novice would be better served purchasing a more expensive kite.

The Trlby kite, a style that is a cross between a modified fighter kite and an Eddy, is a very effective diamond stunter. It is made from durable, high-density polyethylene or ripstop and fiberglass. The Trlby is regarded as one of the better kites for the beginner (either single or in train).

The Peter Powell stunter and Rainbow stunter are both diamond Rogallo Wings. They are all able to adjust in the wind; the stronger the wind, the faster the kite moves. The Powell stunter is an excellent kite for the beginner, but because it has a strong pull, it may be too much for the younger set. The smaller Rainbow stunter is usually sold in stacks (singles are almost impossible to fly) and requires some knowledge of kite flying to handle.

© Francis Hall/Kite Post

© Andre Bagel

© Christopher Bain

Delta and Swept-Wing Kites

Delta (Rogallo Wing) stunters were popular in Europe long before they were available in the United States. One of the earliest versions available in this country was the Skynasaur in 1978. Other types of Rogallo Wings include the Powell Skyraker, Dyna-kites, and the small Hyperkites. These kites are slower than their swept-wing cousins and so are easier to fly.

Swept-wing (Californian) stunters have been around since the early 1980s. They are very efficient flying kites and are able to soar at fast speeds with good control. Most swept-wing stunters are best suited for intermediate to experienced fliers.

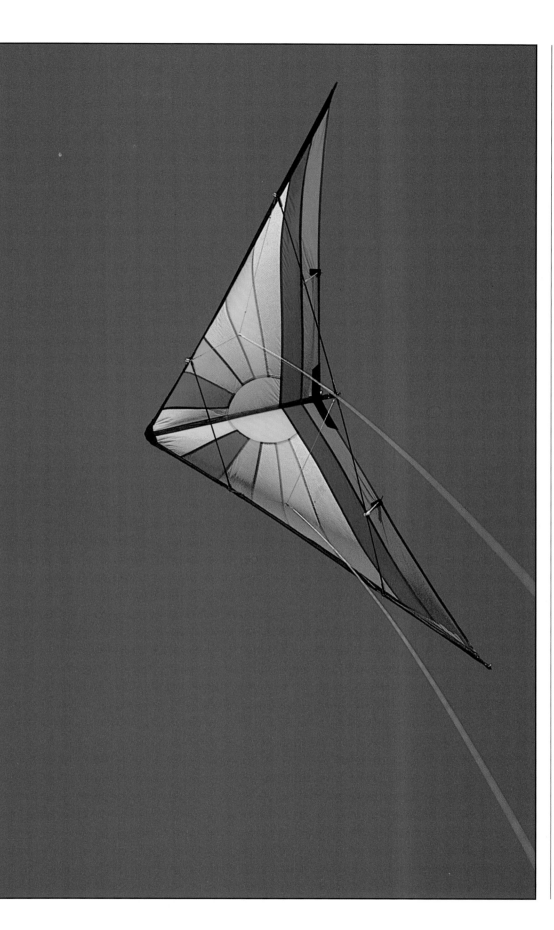

© Andre Baget

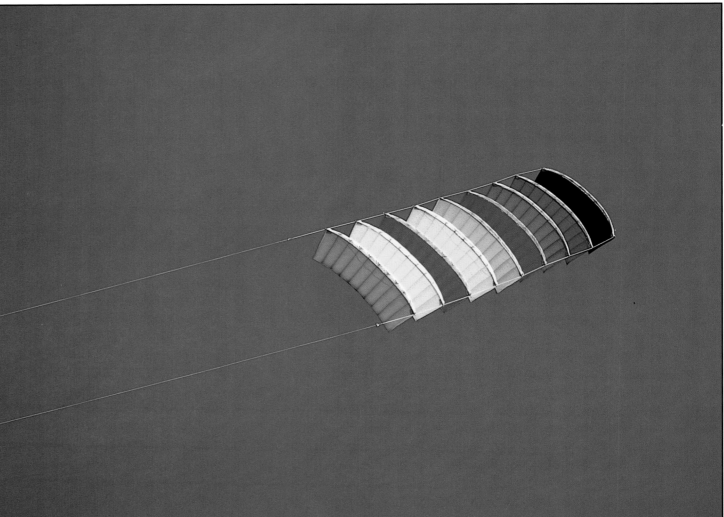

© Francis Hall/Kite Post

Foils

These are wind-inflated kites that have an airplane-wing cross section, or airfoil. The first foil stunt kite was the Flexifoil, also called the "Flying Mattress," which was made in 1976. It was developed from a design school project by Ray Merry and Andrew Jones. One of the Flexifoil's major innovations is a single flexible strut that fits along the leading edge of the kite. There is no bridle, and the two control lines are attached directly to the ends of the strut.

Other foil styles include the Skynasaur C-26 Skyfoil, the Paraflex, Snoopy and the Red Baron, and Kite Innovation's Sparless Stunter. Foils are fast, efficient fliers with a strong pull and are best suited for intermediate to experienced fliers.

© Christopher Bain

Quad-Line Kites

To compare a quad-line (quad-axis) stunter to a dual-line stunter is like comparing a helicopter to a fixed-wing airplane. The first commercial quad-line stunter was the Revolution stunt kite (formally Neos Omega) introduced by Joe Hadzicki in 1988. Hadzicki's design has rewritten the book on controlled flight because it can spin on its center point like a propeller and move backward, forward, and sideways and stop on a dime at the flier's will. Each quad-line handle has two lines that control the kite like a marionette. Unlike a dual-line stunter, a quad-line kite is controlled more by wrist movement than pulling on the control lines.

The Revolution is made up of two sides that can be manipulated independently of each other. The Wright Brothers used a similar technique when they tested their "warp steering" theory by flying a biplane kite on four lines.

Nearly any delta stunter can be flown on four lines, though not as effectively as a kite especially designed for it. This method allows the flier to change the kite's angle of attack in flight. The quad-line delta kite is controlled by adjusting the kite's attitude to the wind, which requires back-and-forth wrist movement. When the kite is in a neutral position, it is possible to steer it with the standard push-pull motion. Many fliers find this technique very frustrating to control the kite.

Other styles of quad-line stunters include Kite Innovation's Quadraflex and Peter Powell's Omni. Quad-line stunters take special skills to fly and are best left to experienced fliers.

■ **ABOVE:** The new sparless Quadrafoil combines the maneuverability of a quad-line stunter with the greater pull and lower relative cost of a traditional parafoil.

■ **LEFT AND BELOW, LEFT:** Robbie Sugarman and Oscar Martinez flying their custom designed "revolution-type" quad stunters at Jones Beach, New York.

© Andre Baget

Stunt-Flying Innovations

With the rise in popularity of stunt kite flying there have been great strides in kite innovations. Though many of the "new designs" can be regarded as little more than the designer flirting with the unusual or, at best, "reinventing the wheel," others have led to a greater understanding of flight. For example, Highly Strung's Checkmate has twin skins that form an inner and outer wing. The low pressure area between the two wings acts as an air-break and benefits flight in strong winds.

About every four years, since the introduction of the Powell Skymaster (1972), a totally new concept in stunt kites has arrived on the scene. These developments have been brought about by accident, as with the Flexifoil (1976), or through the application of engineering principles, as with the Revolution (1988). What will be "the state of the art" in the future is hard to predict. A number of designers are working with new materials and flight technologies.

It is rumored that a "new" kite, called the Manta Ray, is being developed in the United Kingdom. It is said to have a single (not inflatable) surface that forms an "inverted sled" shape in flight. Like the Flexifoil it has a flexible leading edge and single tow points (no bridle) at the wing tips. The Manta Ray's simple construction may do more to revolutionize kite costs than introduce unique flight concepts.

Trains (Stacks)

Stunters are crowd-pleasers, especially when they're stacked one behind the other. Most stunt kites can be stacked successfully. In the early eighties, the late Steve Edeiken popularized stunt train flying in the United States by marketing stacks of his diamond Rainbow stunters. He used matching ripstop tails for an added visual impact that outlined each maneuver. The advantage of a Rainbow stunter "twelve stack" (twelve kites) is that it is small enough for one person to fly and yet large enough to look impressive.

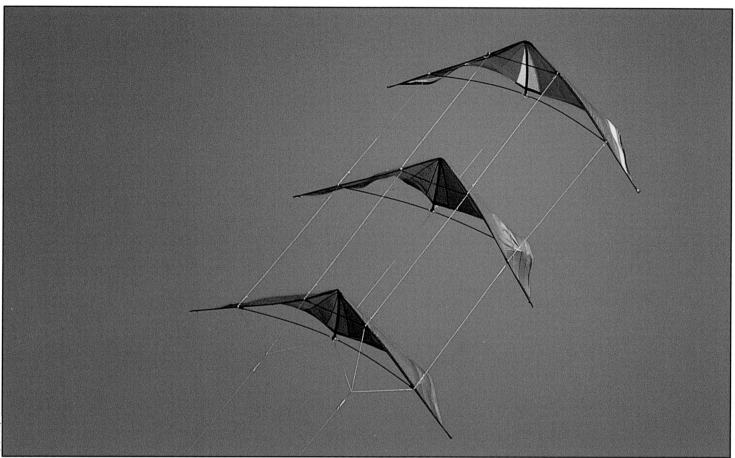

■ **OPPOSITE PAGE:** Top-of-the-Line stunt team flying in close formation, showing what makes them champions.

■ **LEFT:** A stack of three Hawaiian team kites.

■ **BELOW:** A stunt team performing at the East Coast Stunt Kite Championship.

Any large stack, especially large deltas, can be hard to control and requires more strength and skill to handle than an individual kite. Large swept-wing stunters provide the most pull, and they react immediately to your steering maneuvers, even in light to moderate winds. Many fliers seem to be affected by the feeling of power when flying large kites. This can be very dangerous for all concerned. For most fliers the game is not just one of lots of power but also one of finesse.

Some fliers have hooked up boats or land vehicles to harness the energy of their trains of kites. This concept is not new; it dates back at least to 1822 when George Pocock hitched a carriage to a train of steerable kites.

Team Flying

This technique has caught the imagination of a large section of the stunt-flying community. Though team flying is more difficult than flying alone, it is not as hard as

many people imagine. In order for a team leader to coordinate a group's kite maneuvers, each team member flies his or her kite on a different length of line. A leader flies his or her kite on the longest line (for example, 110 feet [33 m]), calls out all maneuvers, and is responsible for keeping the kites away from any potential hazards or collisions. The leader also has to keep an eye on the other kites, each of which is on a line that is 5 feet (1.5 m) shorter than the next person's line, making sure that they are lined up and ready for the next maneuver. Because the kites are on progressively shorter lengths of line to stay out of the air wake of the kites that follow, they travel different distances, which means they have to be tuned to travel at different speeds.

Solo (Dog Stake) Flying

The American kite-flying expert Lee Sedgwick has popularized the technique of "dog stake" flying by including it in his innovative stunt routine. To musical accompaniment, he controls his kite as if he is doing a slow dance with it.

The idea is to fly your kite downwind and to interact with its movements. The flying lines run upwind, through a stake in the ground, and back to the kite. An inherent challenge to this technique is that when you pull the left line, the kite goes right. To overcome this reverse effect, some fliers change lines to the opposite hand.

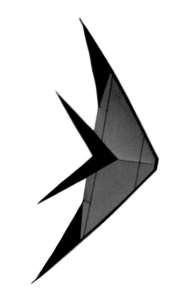

Ultralight Stunters

These kites are generally modified versions of popular swept-wing stunters, but they can be custom-made kites. Some suppliers have ultralight strut kits so that fliers can make their own modifications.

An ultra-light stunter can be flown in a breeze as low as 3 miles per hour (5 kph). Because these kites are built so light that they break easily, and special flying techniques have to be mastered, they are best left for the experienced flier.

Dual-Line Accessories

LINES. Many inexpensive stunt kites come complete with lines and handles. If your particular kite doesn't come with lines, talk to your retailer for advice. A mistake often made by a novice is to try to save money on flying line. The line quality should match the performance level of your kite; use good-quality, low-stretch line. This doesn't mean you should spend forty dollars on line for a twenty-dollar kite. But you can . . . and it works!

The best guide for a line's weight, or test strength, is the manufacturer's specifications for your particular kite. If you use a heavier line than is recommended, you run the risk of the line being dragged along behind the kite's action. This will result in excessive line slack and a loss in the kite's performance. Experienced fliers often carry lines of several weights for light and heavy winds. This can give them an edge that can be very critical in competition flying. (The use of sleeves for knots can help reduce the required line weight.)

It is a common practice to use fishing snap and swivels to attach the line to the kite. Besides making removal and attaching easier, it will extend the life of your line. There are also other methods, but they will not take the twist out of a line. If you choose to use swivels, make sure that they are of a good quality and slightly stronger than the line's rating.

Also it is advisable not to fly a kite on lines longer than the recommended 100 to 200 feet (30 to 60 m). The longer lines result in a loss of control caused by stretch and wind drag. I prefer to fly my stunters on 75-foot (23-m) lines. The challenge (and disadvantage) is that you need to make quicker responses. Even though the kite is

© Andre Bagel

OPPOSITE PAGE: Lee Sedgewick flying his ultralight stunter through a dog stake, which places the kite next to the flier.

LEFT: Innovation stunt event with "the man with four arms."

traveling at the same speed as on a longer set of lines, the maneuver distances are smaller. Also, I have a larger choice of flying areas (and more people can fly in an area) because of my smaller rig.

Nylon is the least expensive but also the least desirable line because of its excessive stretching (as much as 30 percent) characteristics. Never use monofilament fishing line for flying kites.

Dacron, either braided or twisted, can be used successfully with smaller kites. Its approximate 14-percent stretch rate will result in some loss of control.

Kevlar, the same material used in bulletproof vests, doesn't stretch much and can increase the speed and precision of a stunter. Its main drawbacks are its cost and

the fact that it can cut through itself. Tying a knot in Kevlar will reduce its strength by 60 percent. This means that all loops should be sleeved or the ends spliced. Furthermore, Kevlar is UV-reactive, meaning that it weakens over a long period of exposure to sunlight, which should not be a problem for most stunt fliers. Kevlar should be used only by experienced fliers because it is so thin and abrasive (and a stunt kite travels so fast) that it can seriously hurt a bystander!

Shanti's answer to the problems of Kevlar for the novice and intermediate stunt flier is Skybond, which is a Dacron-wrapped Kevlar combination resulting in a low-stretch line. Its main drawback is that it is somewhat heavier and thicker (resulting in more drag) than other lines.

Spectra, also known as Dyneema, is the newest high-tech, low-stretch line on the market. Because of its low melting point, it is especially critical that Spectra line doesn't cross another type of line. It is safe for team flying if the whole squad uses the same line type. Spectra is not without its structural weaknesses and is subject to line failure from being dragged on the ground. It also suffers from line "creep," which means a line will lengthen over time and should be checked periodically.

STUNT HANDLES. For stronger-pulling kites it is best to use heavy-duty ABS handles.

SKY CLAW. This is a complete handle-winding system. It is made up of two foam-cushioned handles, used for flying, that fit into a winder for easy line retrieval.

FLIGHT STRAPS. These are grips made from 1- to 2-inch-(2.5- to 5-cm-) wide webbing (some padded) that fit around the wrists. They make for less effort when flying a hard-pulling kite or train but can be dangerous if a flier is unable to release both hands in case of an emergency.

© Christopher Bain (both)

■ **OPPOSITE PAGE:** Waiting for the next event.

■ **ABOVE:** Sky Claw with line.

■ **BELOW:** Anyone can enjoy launching a stunter.

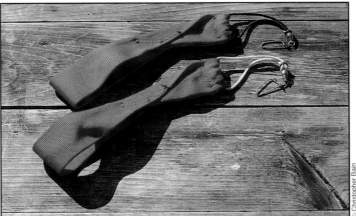
© Christopher Bain

■ **ABOVE, TOP:** This Stinger 1000 rules the beach. **ABOVE, BOTTOM:** Stunt flying can be enjoyed by older children and adults alike. **OPPOSITE PAGE:** These Kite Fanatics practice "Follow the leader," a popular team exercise, with four Phantoms.

Another potential problem can come from improper or extensive use, causing a wrist injury that may require surgery.

HARNESSES. They can be used for strong-pulling kites and trains. They should have quick-release clips for emergencies.

CONTROL BARS. They can give the flier extra control and leverage with trains but can be very dangerous if they get away from a flier. The only control bars that I have seen have all been homemade.

TAILS. Tails can be either tube or ribbon, ranging from 40 to 100 feet (12 to 30 m) in length.

STAKES. These are used for launching a swept-wing kite by yourself. You can use almost anything to hold your handles while you set up your kite. Popular items include screwdrivers and tent stakes. If the flying field is crowded, remove the stakes after each launching, or mark them with a bright flag.

REPAIR KITS. Supplies include: Hacksaw blade (half of one end taped); pocket or utility knife; folding scissors, needle, and thread; spare bridle line; surgical tape (for general repairs) and clear plastic tape (for patching sails); assorted ferrules (for replacing or repairing struts); fishing swivels (tow rings); small tube of instant glue and sandpaper (sandpaper used to clean surface to be glued); marker pen; and tape measure.

VIDEOS. One way of learning flying techniques is to watch the experts in action. Several kite manufacturers sell videos of their kites. There are videos of many events. Contact your local kite store.

Flying a Stunt Kite

Choosing a flying area is a matter of common sense. Basically, the same recommendations apply for flying any kite (see Flying a Kite on page 67). Remember that you don't want to fly downwind of tall objects in order to stay out of the wind shadow, which causes sudden and irregular wind shifts or eddies. A child flying a dime-store delta has a great advantage over the stunt flier. The delta can soar above turbulence, while the stunter must fly within short line constraints, usually below the cause of the turbulence. In a field surrounded by trees, try to fly downwind as much as possible.

WIND RANGE. Your stunter should be rated to show the wind range recommended. Generally, a novice can handle winds of 8 to 20 miles per hour (13 to 32 kph). The ideal wind range for stunt flying is 10 to 15 miles per hour (16 to 24 kph). Do not be misled by the claims of the low end of the wind range on some stunt kites. Kite flying in light winds is difficult and best suited for more experienced fliers.

© Christopher Bain

WIND WINDOW. The "wind window" is the zone downwind of the flier where it is possible to fly a stunter. This zone is limited by the type of wind and its velocity, the kite's efficiency, and the flier's skill level. The stronger the wind, the larger the window.

To find the window's limits, first steer your kite up as high as it will fly. At the edge of the highest point the kite will stall and hover. Next steer your kite to each side to find its stall limits. Again the kite will lose its drive and stall at each side.

You will find the area of most response, or maximum power, directly in front of and level with you. This is where novices should practice flying. As the kite approaches the window's edge, the kite's pull tapers off, and it is possible to steer with small movements with the kite under full control. Many experienced fliers like the challenge of doing stunts at the edges of the wind, where they perform "edgework."

LAUNCHING. Before launching your stunt kite, carefully read all the enclosed instructions. Attach the line to tow points (on bridles) and unwind it. Make sure that the bridles are free and not wrapped around the cross struts. Check that the lines are the same length (with equal tension on both lines) and that there are no crossovers. To avoid pulling on the wrong line, note which line belongs to which handle.

Have your assistant hold the stunter by the sides. On a given signal the kite is released with a slight upward push. With a swept-wing delta your assistant can stand the kite and then move clear. This will allow you to make a snap launch with a quick tug.

PILOTING. Fly your kite up as high as it will go. Keep your hand comfortably at a position a little lower than chest high. Just pull back or push forward and slowly turn the kite and steer it back and forth across the sky. When you pull on the left line, the kite will turn left; when you pull on the right line, the kite will turn right.

LOOPS. Pull one line back and hold it until the stunter has completed one or more loops. Remove the line twists by looping in the opposite direction. To complete a figure eight, just pull the opposite line back so the kite will loop in the other direction.

LANDING. While walking downwind, fly the stunter into the wind, on either side, until it hovers, and guide it to the ground. When you have finished flying, spend a little time removing the flying lines, rolling up your kite, and storing it in a bag. Also check your gear for any wear or potential problems.

■ **BELOW:** The Flexifoil is the world's fastest shuttle kite. It has been clocked at 124 mph (198kph) by a police radar gun.

CHAPTER FIVE

◆

Festivals
and Contests

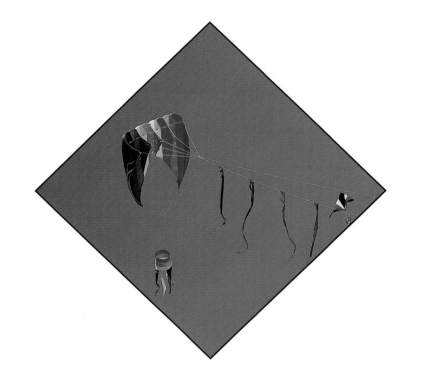

Whenever two or more kite fliers gather, there are grounds for a challenge. With fighter kite fliers this could be a simple game of tag in which they try to disable one another's kites by snaring their tails. Dual-line stunt fliers also can play tag, but the trend is more toward team flying. Fliers can play follow the leader or stage sky ballet routines.

Kite festivals are held throughout the world. Approximately three quarters of these festivals are competitions. The best available calendars of these events are found in the kite magazines listed in the

■ **ABOVE:** Registration desk at a kite festival.

■ **RIGHT:** Giant windsocks act as aerial banners to attract spectators.

Appendix on page 108. For other information on kite events in your area, contact your local recreation department, kite store, radio or television stations, or newspaper. Many kite clubs regularly hold informal kite flies for members. Your local Kitefliers Association can help you with information on clubs in your area.

Kite flying is not as organized as other sports, and there are no standards for conducting kite contests. It seems that every organizer has his or her own ideas. One day you may find yourself planning a kite contest for a scout troop, school, church, or another organization. If so, your best bet is to contact *Kite Lines* magazine for a reprint of its article "Kite Festivals and How to Build One of Your Own." In an attempt to standardize stunt competitions, the American Kitefliers Association and the Stunt Team and Competitive Kiting (STACK) have produced a booklet, "International Kite Competition Rule Book," that is available from your local Kitefliers Association. The following is an overview of types of contests and events available to kite fliers:

Competitions

Comprehensive judging is the method of choice for many kite contests. Either contestants file past a panel of judges, or the judges walk among the fliers. This allows others to enjoy flying their kites while the contestants are being judged.

At a typical kite festival, the contestants carry their registration cards and their homemade kites past the judges one at a time. The judges assign points, from one to ten, for design, craftsmanship, beauty, launch, control, and retrieval. The final judging is on flying, and any kite that fails to launch is eliminated. Categories are divided into age groups, and each person enters his or her kite in two categories (only one award per kite). At the end of the day awards are presented to the first three top scorers in each division:

• **Box kites with or without wings and derivatives**

• **Delta kites and derivatives**

• **Flat surface kites with tails, or bowed kites**

• **Figure and novelty kites**

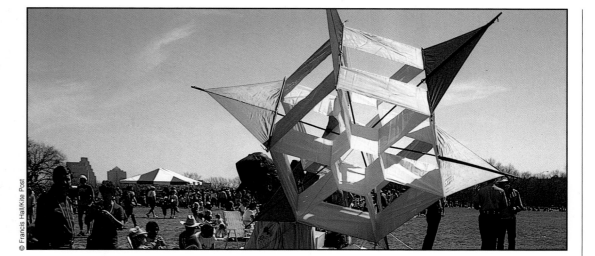

■ **ABOVE:** Waldof hexagonal box kite.

Field Events

Field events are more structured than comprehensive judged competitions, with the day divided up into half-hour segments. The advantage is that contestants can enter as many events as they want. They are restricted by being allowed to have only one homemade kite for each event. Here is a list of typical field events:

1. Highest kite: Contestants release 300 feet (90 m) of line and stand on a designated line. The kite that flies the highest wins.

2. Steadiest kite with a tail at least three feet (.9 m) long.

3. Steadiest kite without a tail.

4. Most active kite.

5. Strongest-pulling kite: Each kite's pull is measured to determine number of pounds.

6. Smallest kite: Entries have at least 25 feet (7.5 m) of line and must fly higher than point of mooring.

7. Most unusual kite: Entries are judged on theme, beauty, and construction. Judges also look for odd, striking, and novel features.

8. Largest kite: Square footage of sail area determines the largest kite, but a kite must be capable of flying five minutes to qualify. Entries conform to a set design: barn door, hexagonal three-stick, Eddy bow, sled, edo, or delta wing.

9. 50-yard (45-m) dash (children 12 and under). Kites carry at least 50 feet (15 m) of line and remain airborne during the whole race.

Awards are presented to the oldest and youngest contestants entering the event. The youngest has to stand unassisted while flying a kite.

Single-Line Kites

FIGHTING KITES. After agreeing to a time limit, two contestants stand in two separate circles, 10 feet (3 m) in diameter, 20 feet (6 m) apart. The kites have to be launched and flown without leaving the circles.

The kites are maneuvered into striking distance, and the bout begins, the object being to cut the other contestant's kite. The loser of each bout launches another kite until the end of the time limit. The person who cuts the most kites is declared the winner.

STUNT COMPETITION

1. The competitor may launch the kite from the ground or from the hand. To receive any points, the

competitor must make the launch and have control over the kite without an assistant.

2. The competitor must exhibit that he or she can change the direction of the kites at will by spinning it in either direction. Each change in direction must be called out.

3. The competitor must position his or her kite in the sky vertically in line with a pole specified by the judges. The poles are approximately 6 feet (2 m) tall and are erected by the competition committee. The kite must dive vertically and come as close as possible to the pole.

4. The competitor must position the kite at midair flying position. After calling either horizontal left or right, the competitor must move the kite as far as possible to the left or right in a straight, smooth, continuous movement.

5. The competitor must knock objects off each pole with either the kite or kite line. There is a time limit of one minute for each object, with unused time for the first available for the second object.

6. The competitor must land the kite in the landing zone as specified by the judges. Any kite landing and bouncing out will be considered out of the landing zone.

NOTE: A deduction of points is made each time the kite touches the ground, except landing. If a kite is grounded during an event, the judge must stop the clock until the kite has been relaunched.

© Christopher Bain (all)

Stunt Contests

Dual-Line Kites

In stunt events contestants can fly any type of dual-line kite (or trains of kites) as long as the kite can be safely flown in the fields provided. That means very large or very long kite trains are not allowed. Props, apparatus, and kite changing are only permitted in the individual and team innovative events. The scoring is carried out by three to five judges. A scorekeeper receives the scores from the judges and tabulates the results.

The competition flying field is an area at least 200 feet square (18 sq m) and free of obstructions. There are two areas set aside for competitors to wait their turn to compete (stage-in) and to land their kites (stage-out). Also, one or more practice fields are generally provided with access on a first-come, first-served basis. A field director is in charge of directing the activities in the competition field, and a pit boss is in charge of the stage-in and stage-out fields.

If the wind falls to a point where the judges feel that it is inadequate for a flier to compete, the event is recessed until conditions improve (6 miles per hour [10 kph] for novice and junior fliers, 5 miles per hour [8 kph] for experienced fliers, and 3 miles per hour [5 kph] for open classes). Also, if the wind reaches a point that the judges feel that a flier cannot fly safely, the event is recessed until conditions improve (20 miles per hour [32 kph] for novices and juniors and 30 miles per hour [48 kph] for all other classes). Every effort is made to complete an event, which may mean rescheduling it for another time.

Classes

JUNIOR: any dual-line competitor under twelve years of age. Any junior who has won in an event at a major stunt kite contest moves to the novice class.
NOVICE: a beginner in dual-line competition who hasn't won in competition or doesn't feel ready to compete in the experienced class. If the flier has placed as a novice

© Christopher Bain

in three or more stunt competitions, he or she moves to the experienced class.

EXPERIENCED: a dual-line flier who has progressed beyond the novice category. Experienced fliers have good mastery of stunt kite control and have been in previous competitions.

MASTERS (ADVANCED): This class is for those who feel that their flying ranks them among the best.

Teams composed of fliers with mixed skill levels will be ranked by the average. A three-person team with two experienced and one open-class flier may fly in the experienced class. If all the members have the same skill level, then they must fly in their class or higher.

Categories

INDIVIDUAL PRECISION. This category is divided into three to five compulsory figures and thirty seconds to two minutes of freestyle flying. The compulsory figures are designed to test the flier's technical ability. Scores are based on shape, size, and direction of maneuvers and how closely points match the ideal figures. Judges like to see crisp corners, straight lines, and closeness to the ground on the sweep figures. The size of the figure can be as large as possible without touching the ground, but the speed has to be constant.

TEAM PRECISION (three or more fliers). This class is divided into two to four compulsory figures and two to five minutes of freestyle flying. The team compulsory figures are designed to exhibit technical flying ability as a team. They have to demonstrate that the team is proficient in executing all figures. Higher scores are given to those teams whose members trace out the same size figure simultaneously. Judges look at technical flying ability made up of either following, flanking, or opposing moves.

INDIVIDUAL OR TEAM BALLET. The individual or team ballet competition is two to five minutes of free flight to music. A ballet team can be made up of two or more fliers. The judges consider the kite-flying interaction of the members of each team and how suited it is to the music. The music should be appropriate for a kite ballet, having variations in mood and tempo to allow for a creative routine. The movement of the kite should interpret and reflect the music.

INDIVIDUAL OR TEAM INNOVATIVE. The innovative flight event is for fliers who want the opportunity to introduce creative or innovative ideas that are not permitted in other events. Fliers have two to six minutes to execute routines that are new and unusual. Props, apparatus, and dancing or acrobatics are all permitted.

© Joe Gschwind

TEAM DIAMONDS

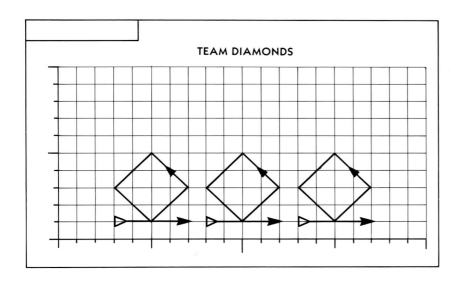

TEAM HAIRPIN

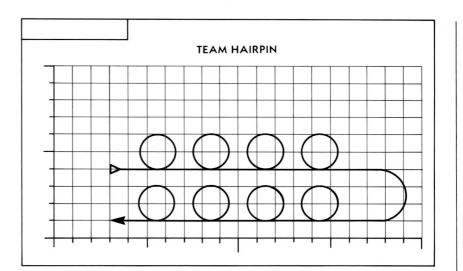

HORIZONTAL THREADS

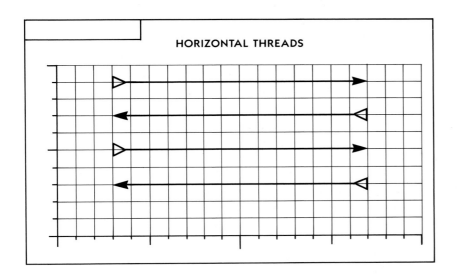

TEAM FIGURE EIGHTS

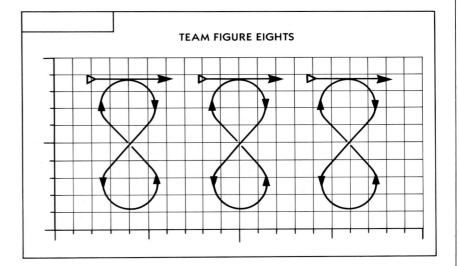

■ These illustrations show several different compulsory maneuvers for three or four team flyers. There are several dozen maneuvers which can be strung together to form a complete routine. These illustrations show four of the fifty maneuvers featured in the newly revised AKA Official Rulebook.

Appendix

International Competitions and Events

United States

Ben Franklin Kite Contest, Philadelphia, PA
Oahu Kite Flying Festival, Honolulu, HI
Kite Flite, Tulsa, OK
Lubbock Kite Fly and Frisbee Fling, Lubbock, TX
Kinetics Kite Fly, Boulder, CO
Memorial Day Kite Festival, Seattle, WA
Maui Kite Festival, Maui, HI
Fourth of July Kite Celebration, Ocean City, NJ
San Diego Kite Festival, San Diego, CA
Cannon Beach Open Fly, Cannon Beach, OR

Australia

Australian Kiting Festival, East Kew, Victoria
Festival of the Winds, Southgate, New South Wales
Victoria Kite Championships, Buninyong, Victoria
Australian Stunt Kite Championships, Elwood,
    Victoria

Britain

Kite Society of Great Britain Annual Convention,
    Weymouth, England
Blackheath Easter Kite Festival, Blackheath, England
Bristol Kite Festival, Bristol, England
Weymouth International Kite Festival, Weymouth,
    England

Canada

Touch the Sky Kite Festival, Ottawa, Ontario
Four Winds Kite Festival, Toronto, Ontario
Down East Annual Kite Festival, Elmsdale, Nova
    Scotia
Pacific Rim Kite Festival, Vancouver, British Columbia

Europe

Ostende Kite Festival, Ostende, Belgium
Le Touquet International Kite Festival, Le Touquet,
    France
Twenty-Second Berlin International Kite Festival,
    Berlin, Germany
Ferrara International Kite Festival, Ferrara, Italy

Kite Organizations

There are many local and international kite-flying groups, associations, and clubs. The following is only a sample. Contact *Kite Lines* magazine for other listings.

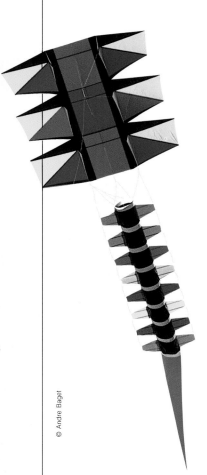

© Andre Bagel

United States

American Kitefliers
   Association
3839 Dustin Rd.
Burtonsville, MD 20866

Washington Kitefliers
   Association
Pacific Science Center
200 Second Ave. North
Seattle, WA 98109

Kite Trade Association
50 First St., Suite 310
San Francisco, CA 94105

Australia

Australian Kite
   Association
c/o Helen Bushell
10 Elm Grove
North Kew 3102
Victoria

Canada

BC Kite Association
c/o Hue Harrison
6058 Crown St.
Vancouver, BC V6N 2B8

Toronto Kite
   Association
c/o John Campton
280 Wellesley St. East
Toronto, ON M4X 1G7

China

Weifang Kitefliers
   Association
42 Shenglis St.
Weifang City
Shandong Province
People's Republic of
   China

© Christopher Bain

England

STACK
78 Dongola Rd.
Tottenham
London
NI7 6EE

British Kite Flying
    Association
P.O. Box 35
Hemel, Hempstead
Hertfordshire, HP2 4SS

Germany

Drachen Club
    Deutschland
Postfach 10 17 07
W-2000 Hamburg 1
Germany

New Zealand

New Zealand Kitefliers
    Association
9 Kenef Road
Paremata, Wellington

France

Cerf-Volant Club de
    France
Boite Postal 186
F-75623, Paris

Japan

Japanese Kite
    Association
c/o Masaaki Modegi
Taimeiken, Nihonbashi,
    1-12-10
Chuo-ku, Tokyo 103

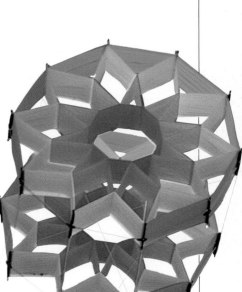

Kite Magazines

Stunt Kite Quarterly
P.O. Box 468
Manastee, MI 49660

American Kite
480 Clementina St.
San Francisco, CA 94103

Kite Lines
8807 Liberty Rd.
Randalltown, MD
  21133–0466

Kite Stores

United States

Flights of Fancy
3901 Old Seward Hwy.,
  Suite 12E
Anchorage, AK 99503

The Kite Korner
520 W. Sheldon St. #4
Preston, AZ 86301

Into the Wind
1408 Pearl Street
Boulder, CO 80202

Kites of Boston
Faneuil Hall
8 N. Market
Boston, MA 02109

Kitty Hawk Kites
Waterside Mall
333 Waterside Dr.
Norfolk, VA 23510

Australia

Skytes
The Boardwalk
Breakfast Creek
Brisbane, QLD

Southern Cross Kite
  Company
92 Kingsbury St.
Norman Park, QLD

Highly Strung Kites
51 Glenhuntly Rd.
Melbourne, Victoria,
  3184

Canada

Kites on Clouds
131 Water St.
Vancouver, BC
V6B 4M3

Touch the Sky
  –Harbourside
207 Queens Quay W
Toronto, ON
M5J 1A7

Ahead of the Game
201-10 St. NW
Calgary, AB
T2N 1V5

Paint the Sky Kite Co.
293 Bay St., Station
  Mall
Sault Ste. Marie, ON
P6A 1X3

Touch the Sky
  –Harbourside
207 Queens Quay W.
Toronto, ON
M5J 1A7

England

Apex Kites
7 Early Common 3
  Bridges
Crawley, West Sussex

Flying Colours
9 Wharf Rd. Frimley
  Green
Frimley, Camberley

Malvern Kites
The Warehouse
  St. Ann's Rd.
Great Malvern,
  Worcestershire

The Kite Company
12 Dalston Rd.
Bristol BS3 1QQ

Europe

Drachenladen
Munsterstrabe 71
4000 Düsseldorf 30
Germany

Alviola Kites
Via Case Nuove 3
02034 Montopoli,
  Sabina (Ricti)
Italy

Der Spieler
Haupstrasse 106
CH-4102 Binninigen
Switzerland

© Andre Baget

111

Bibliography

American Kitefliers Association. *AKA/STACK International Stunt Kite Competition Rules.* 1990, AKA.

Bahadur, D. *Come Fight a Kite.* New York: Harvey House, 1979.

Barwell, E., and C. Bailey. *How to Make and Fly Kites.* London: Cassell and Collier Macmillan, 1974.

Baxter, E. *Kites for Krowds of Kids.* Perth (Aust.): Cats, 1975.

Bin Josoh, and Wan Musa. *Wau Malaysia.* Belia dan Sukan, Malaysia: Kementeria Kebudayaan, 1976.

Botermans, J., and A. Weve. *Kite Flight.* New York: Holt, 1986.

Brummitt, W. *Kites.* New York: Golden Press, 1971.

Bushell, H. *Make Mine Fly.* Melbourne: Australian Kite Assoc., 1977.

Dyson, J. and K. *Fun with Kites.* London: Angus and Roberts, 1976.

Consumer's Guide. *Create-a-Kite.* New York: Simon and Schuster, 1977.

Fowler, W., Jr. *Kites: A Practical Guide To Kitemaking and Flying.* New York: Ronald Press, 1953.

Fujino, A., and B. Ruhe. *The Stunt Kite Book.* Philadelphia: Running Press, 1989.

Gallot, P. *Fighter Kites.* New York: St. Martin's Press, 1989.

Gomberg, D. *Stunt Kites.* Salem, OR: Cascade Kites, 1988.

Greger, M. *Kites for Everyone.* Richland, WA: Self-published, 1984.

Hargus, A., III. *The "No Secrets" Handbook of Dual-Line Stunt Kites.* Self-published, 1989.

Hart, C. *Kites: An Historical Survey.* New York: Praeger, 1967.

Hart, C. *Your Book of Books.* London: Faber and Faber, 1964.

Hayman, F. *Kids and Kites K–3.* Vancouver, B.C.: Teachers Federation, 1975.

Hiroi, T. *Kites, Sculpting the Sky.* New York: Pantheon Books, 1978.

Hosking, W. *Flights of Imagination.* Washington, D.C.: National Science Teachers Assoc., 1987.

Hosking, W. *Kites: Aussie Style.* Houston: Self-published, 1984.

Hosking, W. *Kites in the Classroom.* American Kitefliers Assoc., 1988.

Hosking, W. *Kites of Malaysia.* Kuala Lumpur: Malaysian Airline System, 1990.

Hosking, W. *Wil Bear's Kite Book.* Houston: Self-published, 1988.

Ito, T., and H. Kamura. *Kites.* Tokyo: Japan Pub., 1979.

Jue, D. *Chinese Kites.* Tokyo: Tuttle, 1980.

Marks, B. and R. *Kites for Kids.* New York: Lothrop, Lee & Shepard, 1980.

Moulton, R. *Kites.* London: Pelham Books, 1978.

Mouvier, J. P. *Kites.* Paris: Collins, 1974.

Newman, L. and J. *Kite Craft: The History and Processes of Kite Making Throughout the World.* New York: Crown, 1974.

Newnham, J. *Kites to Make and Fly.* New York: Puffin, 1977.

Pelham, D. *The Penguin Book of Kites.* New York: Penguin, 1976.

Saito, T. *High Fliers.* Tokyo: Japan Pub., 1969.

Streeter, T. *The Art of Japanese Kites.* New York: Weather Hill, 1974.

Sung-Su, C. *The Survey of Korean Kites.* Seoul: Korean Books, 1958.

Thomas, B. *The Complete Book of Kites.* New York: Lippincott, 1977.

Thornburn, N. *Super Kites II.* Self-published, 1983.

Toy, L. *Flight Patterns.* San Francisco: Sky High Press, 1984.

Wagenvoord, J. *Flying Kites.* New York: Collier, 1969.

Yolen, W. *The Complete Book of Kites and Kite Flying.* New York: Simon and Schuster, 1976.